First Bull Run, 1861

Knight's Battles for Wargamers
Introduced by Brigadier Peter Young, M.A., D.S.O., M.C.

First Bull Run, 1861

PETER DAVIS and H. JOHN COOPER

New York City
1973

First Bull Run, 1861
Copyright © 1971 by Charles Knight & Co. Ltd.
ALL RIGHTS RESERVED

For information write to:
Hippocrene Books, Inc.
171 Madison Avenue
New York, N.Y. 10016

First published in Great Britain in 1971 by
Charles Knight & Co. Ltd.
11/12 Bury Street, London EC3A 5AP

First published in the United States in 1973
ISBN 0-88254-210-9

Printed in Great Britain

Contents

		Page
Introduction by Brigadier Peter Young		vii
Preface		xi
Chapter I	The Stage is Set	1
Chapter II	The Battlefield	9
Chapter III	The Commanders and their Plans	17
Chapter IV	The Blow Falls	27
Chapter V	The Confederate Counter	37
Chapter VI	The Triumphant South	48
Chapter VII	The Falls of Chance	55
Appendix I	Notes on Chapters	60
Appendix II	Orders of Battle	63
Appendix III	Arms	68
Appendix IV	Dress	73
Appendix V	Rules	78
Appendix VI	Re-enactment	80
Appendix VII	Bibliography	95

Maps

		Page
Map 1	The American States at the outbreak of the Civil War	2
Map 2	The geographical features and railways of eastern Virginia, 1861	4
Map 3	The disposition and movements of forces, July 1861	7
Map 4	The battlefield area	10
Map 5	The Bull Run line (diagrammatic)	15
Map 6	The Confederate position behind Bull Run, 20th-21st July 1861	22
Map 7	The Confederate position behind Bull Run (diagrammatic)	22
Map 8	McDowell's plan	25
Map 9	Movements of brigades during the battle (diagrammatic)	28
Map 10	Jackson's "Stone Wall"	34
Map 11	Positions of Ricketts, Griffin and supports near Henry House	40
Map 12	The Confederate flank attack	42
Map 13	Map of the table	81
Map 14	Generalised map of essential features for setting up Wargame table	82
Map 15	Opening stages of the re-enactment	86
Map 16	The Union assault	89
Map 17	The end of the game	93

Introduction

by
Brigadier Peter Young, D.S.O., M.C.[1]

MAN is an aggressive and competitive beast. Perhaps this accounts for the current popularity of War Games — even though they are not usually played for money.

In planning their battles and campaigns wargamers have a choice. They can either fight purely mythical wars, or they can take an historical situation and fight on from there. In this series we attempt to cater for those interested in making an actual battle the basis of their strife.

In this series it is our intention to present the wargamer with all the data essential so that he may deploy his formations in such a way as to represent the assets of the two sides when they went over the Start Line.

The series as planned at present ranges from Oudenarde (1708) to Gettysburg (1863), a period when armies consisted, broadly speaking of Horse, Foot and Guns, with, by modern standards, rather rudimentary staffs and services. Despite the introduction of the rifle during most of the period Brown Bess, or her equivalent, was the main infantry weapon. It follows that a wargamer with a well thought out series of rules for the Napoleonic period[2] will be fairly much at home in fighting all the battles described in the series. But while I personally feel that battles of this period lend themselves best to re-enactment on the table top, I confess I would like to see the series expand to take in the odd mediaeval battle, and others as late as the South African War, and even later. Long range artillery and rifles, machine-guns, mines, barbed wire, gas and atomic weapons have done much to turn warfare into a vulgar brawl, but nevertheless there are situations in modern wars which are well worth wargaming.

---

[1] Brigadier Peter Young introduces the series, he has not edited this particular title and the views, etc. expressed in the book are entirely attributable to the Author.
[2] One such set is detailed in *Charge! Or how to Play War Games*, by Brig. Peter Young and Lt. Col. J. P. Lawford, Morgan-Grampian, London, 1967.

Examples are the action at Huj in Palestine (8 November 1917) and the Vaagso raid (27 December 1841) to name but two rather minor actions, which have been adapted to make lively war games. But it is not a bad idea when refighting these modern actions to fight them with the troops and the rules of the Napoleonic Age. Part of the interest of a War Game is to see both sides deployed in serried ranks, with practically every unit present on the table. Modern warfare with its long range weapons, wide intervals and use of cover is far less picturesque than that of the musket period when the foot still fought shoulder to shoulder and the cavalry charged knee to knee.

Readers of this series will find that almost every wargamer has his own set of rules. I do not think this matters very much so long as the range of weapons, and the distance covered in a move is realistically worked out. I have only one bee in my bonnet, which is that elaborate Morale rules are a waste of time. Morale is in the mind of the wargamer himself, for ultimately a war game is a duel between the two opposing generals themselves. Do not let them hide their deficiencies behind the alleged failings of their metal or plastic followers!

In choosing a battle to reconstruct it is not necessary — nor would it often be possible — to select a battle where both sides were equal. Rather, I believe, should one look for battles, like Vimiero (21 August 1808) where both sides were well matched but somewhat dissimilar. At Vimiero Wellesley outnumbered Junot by 17 to 13, but the latter's superiority in cavalry and artillery should have redressed the balance, had he been a match for his opponent in tactical skill.

	The British & Portuguese WELLESLEY	The French JUNOT
Infantry	16,312	10,400
Cavalry	240	1,950
Gunners	226	700
Guns	18	23 or 24
	16,778	13,050

The British had eight infantry brigades and some 2,000 Portuguese auxiliaries, none of whom were in fact engaged. There was no divisional organization. The French had six infantry brigades, organized in two divisions, as well as a small cavalry division. For the purposes of reconstructing this battle one may ignore the division and fight the battle with the brigade as the basic unit or formation. A reasonable arrangement would be to scale down the two armies in this way.

	BRITISH	FRENCH
Infantry	162	104
Cavalry	6	20
Guns	6	8

Add a few staff and you have a situation where both generals may exercise their talents with a very reasonable chance of success. The plan in Jac Weller's excellent *Wellington in the Peninsula* (Nicholas Vane, 1962) will serve very well as a basic for the terrain, though purists may prefer that in Sir Charles Oman's *A History of the Peninsula War* (Oxford, 1903-30).

Players with large forces at their disposal may prefer to double the size of the armies suggested here, but they will probably not find that this will make a great deal of difference. Others will wish to give their light infantry and their grenadiers something of the special characteristics they displayed in those days, and this should be encouraged as adding to the interest of the game, though admittedly making it more complicated.

Some object to war on moral grounds; others complain that it is tedious — 'long periods of boredom, punctuated with short periods of intense fear'. As one who has never found it boring either in fact or fiction, I commend this series if only because men do better to cut throats in theory rather than in practice.

If I might be permitted one word of advice at parting it would be this. Be careful in your selection of opponents. Obviously you should choose someone whom you fondly imagine to be rather less skilled than yourself, though good enough to extend you. But this, of course, is the secret of enjoying any game! More important is it to select someone of genial temper, who understands the rules but is the anthithesis of the Barrack Room Lawyer. Then sweet Reason will prevail and long hours of contented manoeuvring will lie before you!

Peter Young

Preface

THE bare buttocks of the captain shone pink in the summer sun as, with kilt up to his waist, he dashed in pursuit of a chicken to the cheers of his company and the amusement of the onlookers. Amid such laughter and indiscipline the Cameron Highlanders were marching to battle. They were not, however, soldiers of the Queen who were marching along the dusty road from Washington that day in 1861 but were members of the 79th New York State Militia which was trudging its way to defend the Union of the States. Their mood was one of holiday and their uniform gay with diced glengarry and coloured epaulettes though almost all had abandoned the kilt for the regulation blue trousers, but their gaiety was soon to disappear and their military splendour to be revealed for its superficiality.

Strung out along the road were other units of McDowell's Army of the Potomac which was comprised almost entirely of Militia and very raw volunteers whose dress was as colourful and varied as its discipline was lax and its training insufficient. Soon the marching troops were covered with the dust that rose in great clouds from their own feet and from those of the sweating horses which hauled along the guns and waggons which accompanied each division. Also sweating were the regular troops in their dark blue tunics and shapeless kepis, and whose efficiency had fallen with the abrupt departure of many of their officers to fight for the Rights of the States. The United States Marine Corps were there in the column but of this now famous Corps only one battalion was present, and Major John G. Reynolds, who commanded the 348 officers and men, had little cause for confidence. Only five of his officers and nine NCO's had any experience and none of the men had more than three weeks of training. The Militia units in grey or blue, or even the gaudy and impractical dress of Algerian Zouaves, were in little better state but everywhere morale was high as they moved along the twenty-five miles (40 km) to Centreville where they were to concentrate.

The air of picnic suggested by the march was heightened by the presence of smart members of Washington society who rode out, dressed in frock coats and beribbonned gowns, in their elegant carriages to watch the ensuing spectacle as if it were an afternoon's entertainment. The Union troops knew exactly what was going to happen. They were going to find the rebels, then they were going to fight them and beat them and then they would march to take Richmond and then the War would be won. What they did not know was that the battle to which they were marching, and in which they were to shew great gallantry, would be the beginning of the most terrible fratricidal strife in the history of North America; a war which was to cause such a social, political and economic upheaval that its scars are still to be observed today on both the physical and spiritual life of the Union over which it was fought.

The First Battle of Bull Run — also known as First Manassas — has aroused much interest because of its unusual characteristics. In 'Great Military Battles', Bruce Catton writes:

"The battle was one of the strangest encounters in modern warfare. Fought by two almost completely untrained armies, it ended with one army completely routed and the other so disorganised that it could not exploit its victory effectively. It had little military significance except that it forced the American people to see the hard realities of a war which they had begun in a mood of romantic enthusiasm."

The fact that both commanders contemplated an envelopment of the other's left flank does not hide the fact that there were many other possibilities for manoeuvre. The authors have been interested in this battle for some time now and have several times reconstructed it as a Wargame to try out their theories. Their object in this book is to give an accurate description of the battle and its immediate result at the same time trying to shew how it can be reconstructed on a table-top.

In their research for this book the authors have come to the conclusion that the majority of historians who have recounted this battle have seemed content to follow their predecessors. There is a paucity of detailed description but as much evidence as possible has been critically re-examined and prime sources have been consulted whenever available. As a result of this, some conclusions not generally accepted have been reached. It may be that further research into prime sources will render these conclusions untenable, but the authors feel that wherever they have strayed from the paths of orthodoxy, then they have presented a fair case for so doing.

In describing events, the general pattern set by other writers has not been followed. For instance, a detailed account of the Union retreat and the incident of the damaged caisson blocking the Cub Run Bridge have been omitted as it is felt that these form part of the aftermath and are not directly relevant to the battle and its decision. Conversely the events on the Confederate right have been treated in much more detail than usual. Finally because of the needs of the Wargamer the geography and the terrain is also described in detail.

The authors' reasons for choosing this battle are varied. Militarily it was, as Bruce Catton has said, of little importance. Strategically it is claimed to be important because it is supposedly the first strategic movement of troops by rail but this honour definitely belongs to Napoleon III's flank march in Italy, 1859, before Magenta. The prime reason for choosing it is that it makes for a good Wargame re-enactment. The area over which the major fighting took place is small and contains well-defined terrain features. The number of troops involved is also small and so representation down to battalion level is possible. The battle also resembles a Wargame most strikingly in this; the commanders, like Wargame commanders, start the engagement with full units which have suffered no effective losses and with morale neither unduly elated by victory nor jaded by defeat in previous encounters. Perhaps, also, we might compare the Wargamer recreating a large action for the first time with the Generals at Bull Run who were totally inexperienced in the handling of large bodies of men. Thus Bull Run was chosen.

The authors would like to take this opportunity to thank all those who have helped them in any way. Especial thanks are due to: The Commanding Officer and the Senior Education Officer (Major David Turner, R.A.E.C.) of the Infantry Junior Leaders' Battalion for permission to use the Wargames Hobby Room for the re-enactment.

The Army Library Service for help in supplying reference works.

Ernest Owen, Esq., of Virginia, for his help with the terrain description.

Messrs. Airfix Ltd. for providing us with the large number of their excellent figures needed for our re-enactment.

Donald F. Featherstone, Esq., for information supplied.

All the members of the Infantry Junior Leaders' Battalion Wargames Group who have helped in many ways, but particularly to Junior Privates Keith Calvert, Gary Lewis, Peter Leadbetter and Stephen Matthews.

Terry Bebbington for help with rules.

Jack Coggins, of Hill Church Pa., not only for allowing us to use material from *Arms and Equipment* but also for providing us with additional artillery information.

Finally our especial thanks must go to our wives who have supplied us with encouragement and sustenance whenever needed.

Oswestry, November, 1970

CHAPTER I

The Stage is Set

BECAUSE Washington, the American capital, lies one State south of the Mason-Dixon Line and on the banks of the river which marks the northern boundary of Virginia and because there was a popular demand for an early invasion of that State by the city's more chauvinistic inhabitants, it was, perhaps, inevitable that a major battle should take place in the northern part of Virginia during the summer of 1861. Minor actions in the tumbled ranges of West Virginia had already served to whet the martial appetites of all — except those who had suffered directly — as well as to add point to the argument that the real decisions would be made on the coastal plains of East Virginia.

The geography of the settled part of the United States of America determined that the Civil War should be fought in two separate theatres. The Appalachian Mountains slashed through both North and South and New Orleans was probably more important to the Confederacy than Richmond, but the very fact that the latter was chosen as the capital is a measure of the importance that was attached by all Southerners to the pre-eminence of the 'Old Dominion'. Virginia's laggard decision, on 17th April to join the Confederacy and the choice of Richmond as the Southern capital on 21st May, determined much of the strategy of the subsequent fighting. This was not only true of the first real trial of strength along Bull Run but also of the last sad campaign which led to Lee's surrender in 1865. Virginia was the Belgium of the disunited States, the cockpit of the Civil War, and though Grant's exertions along the Mississippi and Sherman's strategic moves between Chattanooga and Bentonville were to force the Confederacy to its knees, it is significant that only the fall of Richmond and the pitiful retreat which followed brought an end to the fight.

In this respect, Lincoln and others were right to believe that their aim must be to take the Southern capital and in 1861 there were few Northerners who could imagine that a major route to

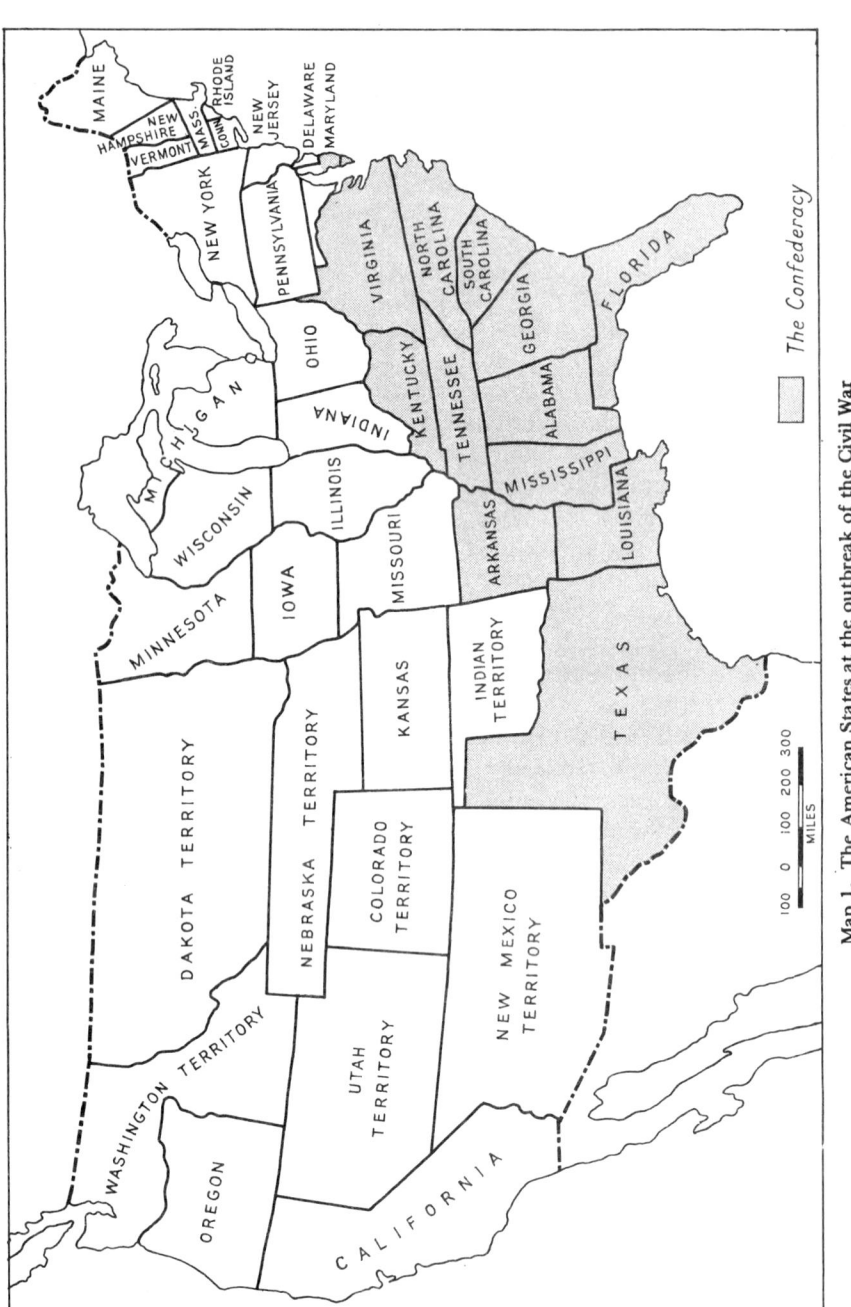

Map 1. The American States at the outbreak of the Civil War

victory would run through Vicksburg and Atlanta. Lincoln was correct, too, in fearing for his own capital. Lee and Jackson in particular correctly diagnosed the Federal nightmare that Washington might be captured, particularly from the direction of Harpers Ferry, and it was not an error that Johnston should be sent to reinforce the rather tentative hold which his fellow-Virginian, Jackson, had laid on the Shenandoah Valley. Meanwhile, Beauregard, 'Hero of Sumter',[1] was given control of the main southern approaches to Washington where he began to make "brilliant and comprehensive but essentially impracticable" plans.

It might have been better for the Union strategists had Lincoln moved his government to New York or Philadelphia. Instead, and in spite of his having to suspend *habeas corpus* throughout Maryland, he gathered into Washington and its environs a host of three-month volunteers who were confidently expected to march down to Richmond and snuff out the "rebellion" within a few weeks. Perhaps it was because the politicians and newshawks were daily rubbing shoulders with the saviours of the nation, visiting their swelling camps and exchanging with their officers the extravagant wisdom that is born of ignorance that their ebullient optimism was soon transformed into a firm conviction of invincibility. It seemed that "On to Richmond" could be accomplished as easily as it was uttered. Who could possibly withstand the military muscle of the Atlantic shore cities, of the Pennsylvania coal-towns and the farms and forests of all the North-Eastern States which was now flexed along the banks of the Potomac? The conviction of early victory grew, and though that old warrior, Winfield Scott, General in Chief of the U.S. Army — still wise despite his seventy-five years — knew that an army needed training more than fervour, he was ridiculed for his beliefs by the majority of Northerners who thought that Richmond must fall within weeks. Only Beauregard and Johnston barred the way.

The strategy adopted by Lincoln and Scott was simply based on the assumption that once the railroad junction at Manassas came under Federal control it would allow them to move troops easily and swiftly to the Shenandoah Valley while the junction itself would serve as a base for movement along the Orange and Alexandria Rail Road into the heart of Virginia and eventually to Richmond. But first, Beauregard had to be brushed aside.

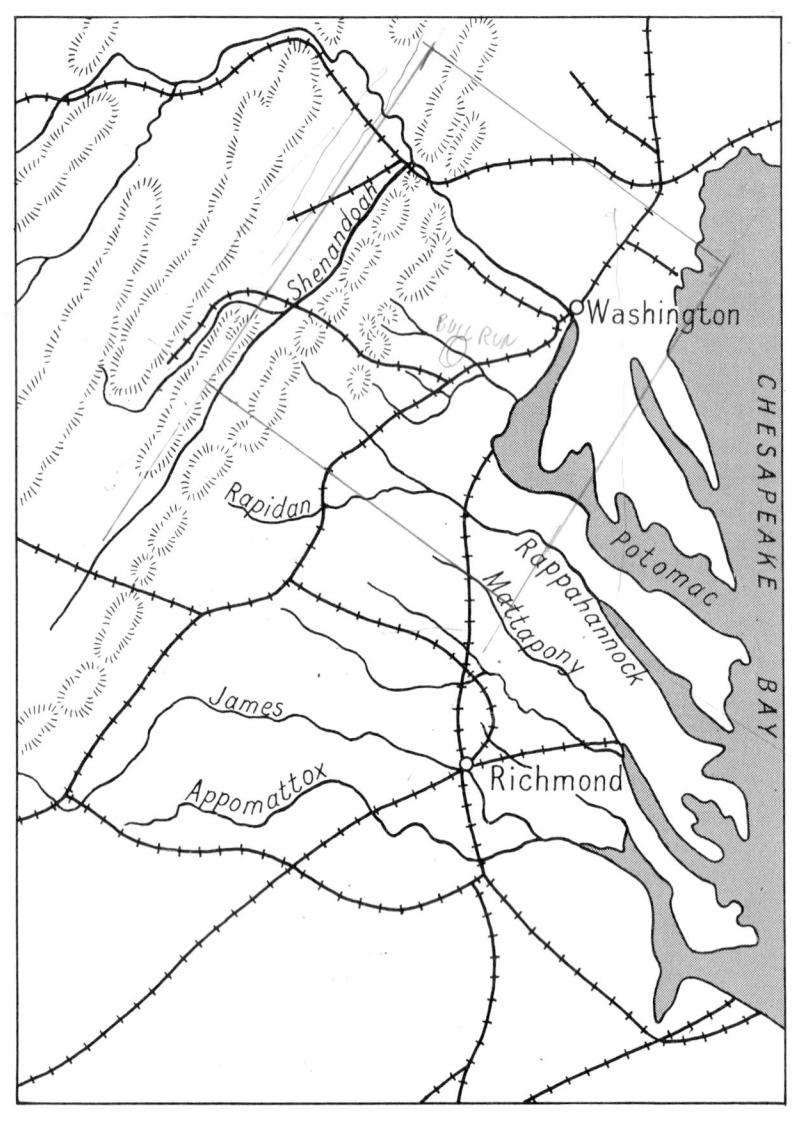

Map 2. The geographical features and railways of eastern Virginia, 1861

There was no immediate need to tackle Johnston provided that he could be induced to remain in the wings. Some diversion, therefore, must be provided to keep Johnston's 12,000 men in the Valley so that they would not join Beauregard's 20,000 about Manassas. How McDowell dealt with the latter was his business. A former instructor in Tactics at West Point, he seemed competent enough, and if his troops were somewhat raw then so were their opponents. In any case — and this is a salient fact — many of the ninety-day volunteers would soon come to the end of their engagements. A short and relatively easy campaign concluded they would be able to return triumphantly homewards with the thanks of their President and tales for their grandchildren.

Joseph Eggleston Johnston, "a temperamental enigma", had been given the Shenandoah Valley command in May. Almost immediately, he had withdrawn from the tactically untenable Harpers Ferry. This gap town had been occupied by Jackson who seems to have agreed with Lee, the overall commander of Virginia's troops, that an offensive movement into Maryland, cutting the Baltimore and Ohio Rail Road and threatening Washington, might cause more than a little confusion in the capital city. However Johnston, nominally commander of all Confederate troops in northern Virginia, placed himself at Winchester to await developments and to watch old Patterson who was bumbling his hesitant way into the northern Valley. Neither Johnston nor the planners in Richmond could do much more. The Confederacy must await a Federal drive and then use its advantage of interior lines to concentrate and meet it as and when it materialised. There was little danger that the Southerners would be taken unawares as Confederate sympathisers abounded in Washington. In any case, that city's newspapers trumpeted almost every thought that Lincoln, Scott and McDowell had on the subject and it was not long before Davis, Lee and Johnston knew that the Northern thrust would come down the road to Manassas Junction. There were to be no clever innovations, no subtleties like McClellan's 1862 Peninsular plan, no flank marches up the Shenandoah Valley. And West of the Appalachians? Well, there was not much point in worrying about Kentucky or Missouri and it would be a waste of time to study maps of New Orleans or Vicksburg because Richmond would be captured in a few weeks, Jeff Davis and his henchmen would be suing for peace or running through the Carolinas and the Union would be restored almost as though nothing had happened. To be fair to Lincoln's advisers, it should be pointed out that the Richmond strategists also gave little thought to the Mid-West. They too believed that if they could hold Virginia events must lead to a general recognition of the justice of their cause.

As McDowell scurries to make his over-hasty arrangements let us look at the stage and the actors. Take your seat in the Atmospheric Circle high above Chesapeake Bay and gaze out across northern Virginia now illuminated by the spotlight of the sun in July, 1861. From a backcloth of the mazed Appalachian ridges, brush-choked streams are gathered into the wide Potomac which, breaking through towards the coast, collects the Shenandoah from its rich farmland valley. It then winds majestically past Harpers Ferry, through the Blue Ridge and down the rolling plain on our right to empty below Washington into the Bay. To our front and left there is no comparable stream until we see the James, Richmond's river, which pleats the coastal plain all the way from its Blue Ridge Gap to the Navy Yards near Norfolk. Between these, the Rappahannock, the Rapidan, the Pamunkey and others all source on this side of the Ridge and gently crease the rolling Piedmont before widening into the swampy and impassable rias of the coastal plain. Smaller still are a number of dendritic tributaries all so small as to be relegated to the term of "Run" until gathered into their mainstream, the Occoquan. These drain the low Piedmont hills called Bull Run Mountains and the rolling country between the Potomac and the Rappahannock.

The iron road which runs from Washington into the heart of Virginia crosses these runs — first Bull Run, then Broad Run, then Cedar Run — while a branch-line points back along Broad Run and uses its valley to pierce the Bull Run Mountains at Thoroughfare Gap before overcoming the more difficult barrier of the Blue Ridge at Manassas Gap.

Manassas Gap is one of a series which segment the high forested Ridge which would otherwise completely block from our view the ridge and furrow country stretching parallel with, but beyond the Shenandoah.

Lost indeed from our immediate view is McClellan's small Union column at Huttonsville, apparently intent on a march against Staunton in the upper Valley but still beyond the main

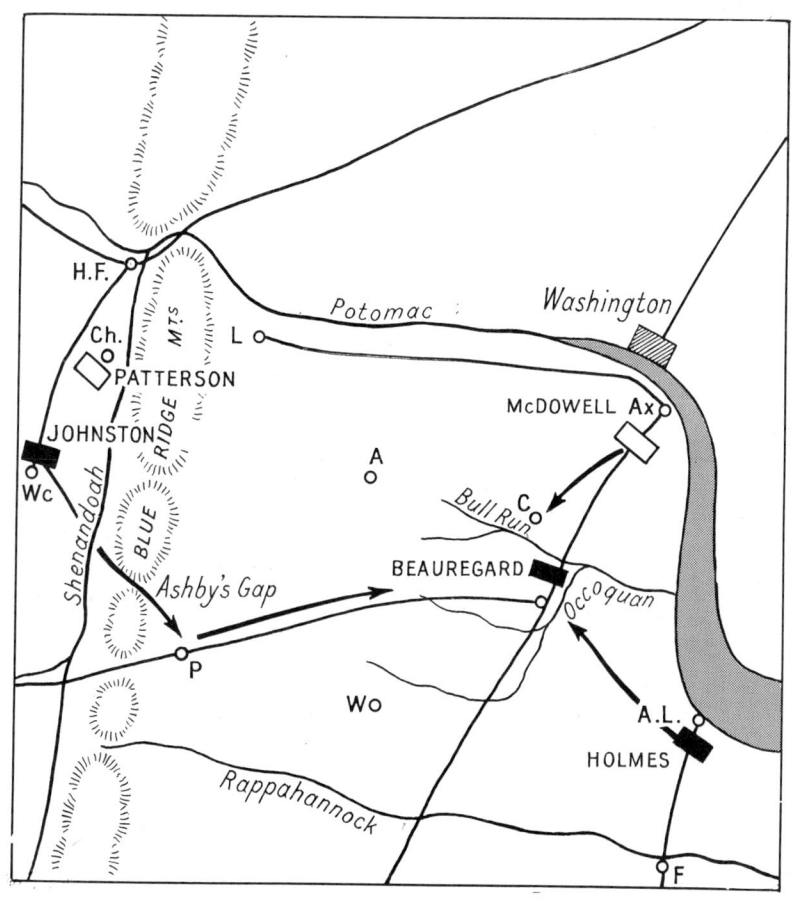

Map 3. The disposition and movements of forces, July 1861 (Confederate forces shown as black squares).

A.—Aldie	C.—Centreville	H.F.—Harpers Ferry	W.—Warrenton
A.L.—Aquia Landing	Ch.—Charleston	L.—Leesburg	Wc.—Winchester
Ax.—Alexandria	F.—Fredericksburg	P.—Piedmont	

Allegheny Ridge. Nearer to us but still deep in the ridge country at Monterey, a couple of fresh Confederate regiments serve as a rallying point for those who have fallen back before McClellan's advance. Still nearer again, in what was to become the "panhandle" of West Virginia, the one glaring defiantly northward and the other gazing back almost sheepishly, stand Johnston and Patterson. The latter has recently moved gingerly across the Potomac from Maryland and his 18,000 men now stand indecisively at Bunker Hill while he telegraphs at length to Washington. Johnston waits at Winchester, nine miles (14½ km) away, with his 12,000, one eye on Patterson and the other on Manassas Gap.

In the foreground, astride Bull Run, Beauregard and his 20,000 look along the Warrenton Turnpike and the Orange Rail-Road towards Alexandria where McDowell is busy. Even nearer to us is a small force of 3,000 Confederates under the North Carolinian, Holmes, guarding the coastal railway landing at Aquia Creek, while far over to our left Fort Monroe, held by about 15,000, Union troops under Butler are faced by small Confederate groups at Yorktown and Norfolk.

Thus the "blind wrestlers of armies" as the curtain rises. It is Tuesday, 16th July, 1861, and McDowell's columns emerge from Alexandria and shake out along the roads towards the Bull Run crossings. Patterson's important force remains immobile at Bunker Hill. Johnston fidgets, not knowing yet that next Sunday's battle has already been given to the Southerners by Patterson's present lack of aggression.

CHAPTER II

The Battlefield

MOST of the Piedmont country of northern Virginia is, in a word, easy.[1] The land surface is seldom broken by any sudden eminence upon which the strategist might seize as a key position, while the lazy windings of its rivers and the no-nonsense directness of its roads testify to the lack of very steep gradients. From the military point of view it is a country of river lines and here, as in the Mississippi lowlands, it was in terms of rivers that the Civil War generals formulated their plans. Thus, when McDowell began to trudge his as yet unwieldy brigades out of the Alexandria defences towards Centreville it was behind the largest stream in the area that Beauregard prepared to receive the Northern host.

A stream as big as Bull Run would well merit the term "river" in England. At Sudley Springs it is little more than ten or fifteen miles (16-24 km) from its source in the Bull Run Mountains. Immediately below Sudley it collects a major tributary, Catharpin Creek, before it curves east, then south-west and then south-east for a lazy three and a half miles (5½ km) down to the single span Stone Bridge which carries the Warrenton Turnpike across its thirty or forty feet (9-12 m.).

From the Turnpike downstream to the railroad bridge (which Beauregard had now destroyed) at Union Mills the stream repeats the same winding pattern but on a much bigger scale. For two and a half miles (4 km) it flows generally south-eastwards but, soon after collecting the small stream which drains the New Market district on its right, it swings east-north east for some three and a quarter miles (5¼ km) to Blackburn's Ford. South-east to the Union Mills Bridge is another two and a half miles (4 km) of gentle curves but with none so acute as to deserve the name of meander.

Downstream from the Stone Bridge, Bull Run collects a number of tributaries which trickle down from the rolling plateaux on either side and all these side streams enter the

Map 4. The battlefield area

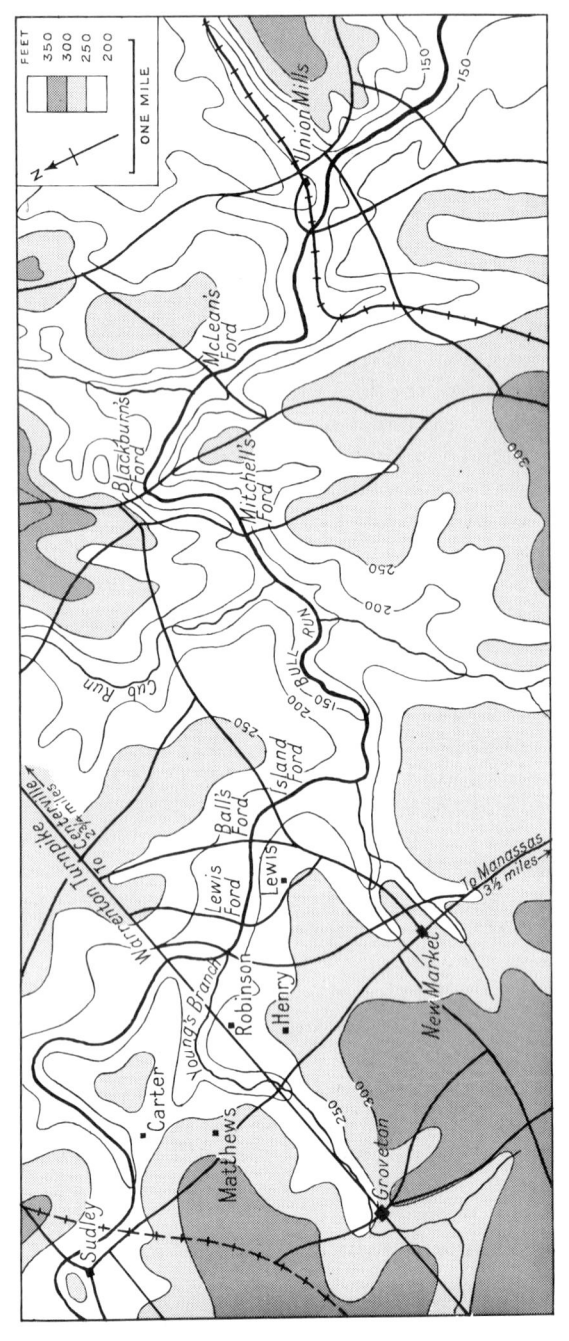

river more or less at right angles to its general south-easterly course. The valleys of two right-bank streams, the New Market Brook and Flat Run, combine to corrugate the landscape between the Manassas plateau — a broad three-hundred foot (91½ m) expanse rising one hundred and fifty feet (45¾ m) above the level of the stream bed and lying about three miles (5 km) south and west of the Run, and the Bald Hill[2] feature of similar height and proportions which lies somewhat closer to the river but five miles (8 km) away to the north-west. Beyond Bald Hill, and separating it from yet a third broad plateau, is the basin of Young's Branch. This small stream drains the area around Groveton and flows generally eastwards before emptying into Bull Run less than half a mile (800 m) below the Stone Bridge.

Thus, the land lying south and west of Beauregard's defence line — three broad stretches of rolling plateau all of roughly the same height which, but for the erosive work of the small tributaries, would have formed a continuous stretch of gently undulating countryside. The valleys which dissect the surface are broad and gently sloped so that they hinder neither the roadmaker nor the few farmers of the district.

Between the valleys, broad undulating spurs reach down from the plateaux towards Bull Run. In the north, an area almost a mile square (2½ sq. km.), edged by Young's Branch and the bend of Bull Run is totally occupied by the wide, gently sloped surface of Matthews Hill (really a spur cut through by a shallow saddle) which tumbles, gradually in the south and east but more severely in the north, down to the rivers. Cutting across the neck of this spur, too unconcerned by gradient to show more than a minor deviation, is the Sudley - New Market - Manassas Turnpike. Locally of some consequence, this road is to figure prominently in the troop movements of the coming battle. It crosses the Warrenton Turnpike one and a quarter miles (2 km) west of the Stone Bridge in the very bottom of the Young's Branch Valley and here, in the angle of the roads, stands the substantial dwelling known as the Stone House.

The Sudley-Manassas Road now cuts deeply into the north-facing slope of our second plateau feature — that topped by Bald Hill — as it climbs on its way to New Market, crossing the necks of the two broad gentle spurs which reach out towards Bull Run. The first of these, crowned by the small Henry farmstead, angles north-eastwards towards the Stone Bridge.[3] The second spur, which trends directly eastward from Bald Hill, is broader than the Henry House Hill and reaches out as though to force Bull Run into a south-easterly course below the Young's Branch confluence. Though heavily clothed with thickets of oak woodland, some of this spur has been cleared and is draped with the wide fields of the Lewis farmstead known as Portici. Between the Sudley Pike and Bull Run a number of roads and tracks swing across this Lewis Spur and down to a series of four fords across the Run itself. One of these, Ball's Ford, carries the old Warrenton, Alexandria and Washington Turnpike. Another, Island Ford, carries a track which parallels the Run as it turns east-north-east and both stream and track lead on to Blackburn's Ford.

It is at Blackburn's Ford that we meet the extremity of the third of the major plateaux which lie to the south of Bull Run. To reach the higher parts of this Manassas Plateau, the Sudley Pike, leaving Bald Hill to the West runs on southwards through New Market until it crosses the Manassas Gap Railroad. At this point it is almost exactly four miles (6½ km) from the Stone House and it is here that the Pike turns south-east to follow the railway for a further two and a half miles (4 km) to the small, but now busy, hamlet of Manassas. The settlement stands more or less at the centre of the plateau and while the railway line, using a small valley, grades gently down the eastern side towards Union Mills, roads take a more northerly course along the crests of two broad spurs which point towards Blackburn's and Mitchell's Fords.

It is immediately remarkable that the sides of these features are much steeper, though far from precipitous, than the sides of the Matthews, Henry and Lewis spurs. The road gradient down to Blackburn's Ford, for example, is in the order of one in six within a few hundred yards of the river. These commanding slopes overlook the crossings which are closest to Centreville only three miles (5 km) away to the north. Little wonder then, that it was here that, upon Lee's advice, Beauregard placed so many of his regiments[4] when McDowell's threat materialised. (Note that, though placed in a good defensive attitude, this concentration was deployed for an attack towards Centreville.) He placed them correctly too for it was here that the Northerner essayed his first crossing of Bull Run.

Centreville nestles close under the highest land in this area — another plateau feature rising to a little over four hundred feet (121 m) near the village itself. From it a broad spur shoulders south-eastwards towards Blackburn's Ford and it is obvious that, but for Bull Run, this feature would form a continuous ridge connecting the Centreville Plateau with its Manassas counterpart. The Blackburn Ford crossing then, is the only obstacle to mar a relatively simple advance along this wide, well-drained feature and no doubt McDowell's reconnaissances soon revealed this fact.

McDowell obviously took note also of the salient features of the landscape in the direction taken by the Warrenton Turnpike out towards the Stone Bridge. Between Centreville and the river this road switchbacks idly for four and a half miles (7¼ km) across Cub Run and its small tributaries, where these flow southwards gathering, eventually, to empty into Bull Run little more than a straight-line mile (1½ km) above Blackburn's Ford. North of the road and facing across Bull Run towards the Matthews spur is a block of plateau similar in height, shape and proportions to those already described. A southward projection of this plateau runs more or less parallel with the river, but is approached by the stream near its extremity in the region of Island Ford. Thus it provides something of a counterpart to the Lewis spur across the river, and between the two lie all four of the fording places where tracks lead up through the timber which edges the Lewis fields on the way to New Market.

Had McDowell plunged straight along the Orange and Alexandria Railroad tracks in his efforts to capture Manassas, then the topography of The Union Mills area would have become as familiar to the historian as that of the Stone Bridge area but, as he did not, only a brief description is given here. As at Blackburn's Ford, the higher ground has not been sufficiently dissected by tributaries to prevent its close approach to the main stream. South of Union Mills, therefore, two portions of the plateau, one on each side of the river, wrap themselves closely around its valley so as to form a constriction. Thus between these and the Centreville-Manassas "ridge" there lies a basin, across the undulations of which trickle a number of tributaries, mainly left bank streams like Little Rocky Run, all emptying into Bull Run between Blackburn's Ford and the Union Mills crossings. In many ways this small basin-like area duplicates the wider basin upstream from Blackburn's Ford and, stretching back up the Bull Run and its tributary valleys as far as Sudley Springs.

The road pattern is that which one would expect to find in an area of scattered hamlets and single farmsteads. Three major thoroughfares have already been mentioned — the Warrenton Turnpike, the Sudley-Manassas Turnpike and the road through Blackburn's Ford which connects Centreville with Manassas. These form a wide and irregular triangle with Centreville, Manassas and the Stone House cross-roads forming its north-east, south and north-west corners respectively. Within the triangle and around its edges a loose mesh of dirt roads and tracks serve the sprinkled farmsteads, their directions determined more by the location of the farms and fords than by the configuration of the land[5].

The main roads built during the "Turnpike Era" (1790-1830) are well drained by side ditches. In width they compare with any medium-sized English country road. They are gravel-covered and do not carry any but minor ruts. On the other hand the minor roads and trackways are little more than farm tracks, powdery with ankle-deep red clay dust during dry periods and almost marshy during time of heavy rain.

During Colonial times much of the north Virginia Piedmont had been quickly settled and brought under cultivation, though it was never as densely populated as, say, the Hudson Valley or Jersey lowlands. The lure of El Dorado lands along the frontier together with the passage of time and the attendant realisation that not all of the Tidewater or Piedmont farms could sustain even pioneer agriculture over several generations meant that much of the land had reverted to Nature. Only the better land was kept under cultivation. Even so, not all of the land had been cleared in the first place, so that by the 1860s a hotch-potch of some virgin oak and much second-growth pine and oak scrub tracts cover the area. Set among these are patches of farmland with scrubby pasture-lands and loosely fenced fields growing corn, tobacco and fodder crops. This is not the magnolia blossom South with large mansions and wide, slave maintained plantations. The land gives only grudgingly and the living it affords is not an easy one.

This "hardness" of the land is especially obvious towards Manassas where brambly thickets and wide stretches of briar-carpeted pine scrub give much of the land the appearance of a wilderness. Further north, the woodland becomes patchy and there are more fields, especially along the Turnpikes and the land around Stone Bridge is well-cleared except along the steeper bluffs. On the other hand, much of the countryside north of the Warrenton Pike is fairly heavily wooded, though there are open meadows along the less steep northern and eastern slopes of the Bull Run valley and there is an unusual air of well-being about the Sudley Mansion estates, farmed by Mr. Cushing, which break the forested lands around Sudley. It is noteworthy that only this Sudley house and the Carter home, which stands near the crest of the Matthews spur, bear the title of Mansion. Other farms and houses in the district are less imposing. Edgar

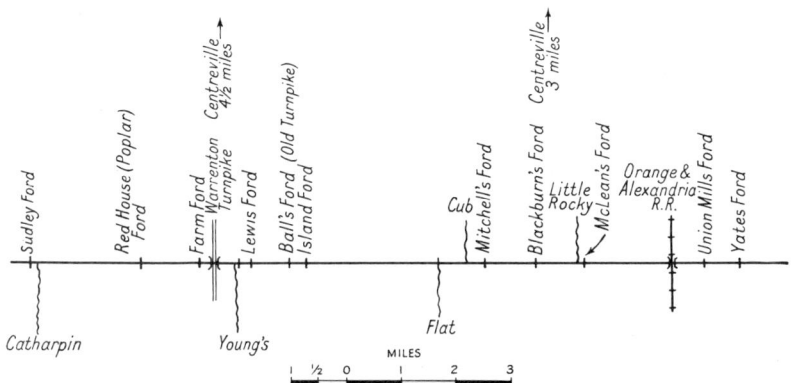

Map 5. The Bull Run line (diagrammatic)

Mathews, Benjamin Chinn and widow Judith Henry's family are run of the mill farmers, not very rich but managing to make a simple, peaceful living from their soil and their houses, like the Stone House and W. Lewis's Portici, are substantial but far from opulent. The Robinson and Van Pelt places resemble English small-holdings. Robinson himself is a free Negro farming the end of the Henry House Hill within the bend of Young's Branch, and his neighbour, Van Pelt, has a few fields within the angle of Young's Branch and Bull Run.

Had Beauregard chosen to stand elsewhere in northern Virginia than here, the first major battle of the Civil War would not have differed generally from that set between Centreville and Manassas. True, if nearer the sea, the field might have been damper; if closer to the Blue Ridge it might have been hillier. But McDowell had the yell of "On to Richmond!" ringing in his ears and so he took the shortest route for a short war. Beauregard meant to stop him along the first real river that lay across that route, and so Bull Run becomes the predominant feature on our table.

CHAPTER III

The Commanders and their Plans

IRWIN MCDOWELL, an artillerist with a French education, had graduated, at the age of twenty, with the position of twenty-third in the West Point Class of 1838. Pierre Gustave Toutant Beauregard, Engineer Officer and scion of the Creole society of Louisiana, had gained second place in the same class. Joseph Eggleston Johnston, their elder by ten years, had served on the frontier and had skirmished against the Seminoles in Florida before they had completed their studies. All three men had served in the Mexican War, where Johnston collected five wounds and three brevets, Beauregard two of each and McDowell one brevet.

By early 1861 Johnston, with prairie cavalry service behind him, was a Brigadier-General and Quartermaster. Beauregard, the Engineer, had opened up some river mouths on the Mississippi Delta and was then opening up the minds of cadets in his capacity as Superintendent of West Point. He was a major and had a promising career before him until he made some indiscreet remarks about secession to one of his cadets. Meanwhile McDowell, also a major, was adding promise to his career by getting to know influential people in the capital where he was serving with Army Headquarters. Made Brigadier-General on 14th May he assumed command of the troops around Washington two weeks later, by which time Johnston and Beauregard had skipped south. On the same day that McDowell received his stars Jo Johnston became a Major-General of Virginia and a Brigadier-General of the Confederacy, after which he moved north again to take command at Harpers Ferry. Beauregard, made Brigadier-General on 1st March, fired on Fort Sumter and was then sent to take command at Manassas.

All three spent a great deal of time during the hot summer days in organising their commands — a task at which they had, of necessity, to work hard. Johnston's problem in the Shenandoah Valley was made somewhat easier as his opponent there was more a politician than a soldier. At Manassas, the *beau sabreur* was having a difficult time, partly because he had more men to organise, but mainly because he was painfully aware that he had not enough men. While it is true that a general cannot know too much about his enemy, the information which filtered into Beauregard's headquarters gave him little confidence. He was able "to receive regularly, from private persons at the Federal capital, most accurate information, of which politicians high in council as well as War Department clerks, were the unconscious ducts." He tells of the Northern Adjutant General's clerk, a talkative fellow, captured on 4th July. He admits the usefulness of the Northern newspapers and we must agree that few generals have been so well served by such a Fifth Column. Certainly few can have been more intimidated by the information it provided (though other Civil War generals, notably McClellan, must be among them) for he found that he was facing an army of at least fifty thousand with "barely 18,000 men with 29 field guns."

In these circumstances it is not really surprising that he called for help. By concentrating almost all the Confederate troops in Virginia, he said, he might strike aggressively around McDowell's "more convenient" flank and cut him off from his Alexandria base. Back in Richmond the plan was looked at and then set aside as impracticable. So, ignorant of the fact that he would eventually be substantially reinforced, he destroyed the Union Mills bridge and issued to his unit commanders a plan for the eventual adoption of a defensive pose along the deep-set Bull Run.

The Confederate Army of the Potomac, now 24,000 strong as the result of drib-drab reinforcements, began to concentrate above the river crossings during the night of 16th July. During that day a short, coded message had been passed by buggy and boat from a house on Sixteenth Street, Washington, down the left bank of the Potomac, across the estuary and into Manassas. This message, telling of the imminence of McDowell's advance, had the effect that fire has on an adventuresome child — a rapid pulling away and a cry. Beauregard's cry was in the form of an earnest telegram calling on Richmond for help and informing the war leaders that, if necessary, their army would be saved by a withdrawal to the Rappahannock.

The cry heeded, Holmes was ordered to move up and Johnston was told that he was to join Beauregard "if practicable". It was practicable, and Beauregard sent trains to meet the Shenandoah brigades. At the same time though, he feared that the concentration "was to go for naught" so he toyed with an alternative plan. In this he proposed that Johnston might march, not to Manassas but via Aldie, at the northern end of the Bull Run Mountains, and onto McDowell's right rear while he, Beauregard, attacked McDowell in front. Fortunately for the Confederates, Johnston took no notice of this suggestion. Beauregard writes: ". . . his (the enemy's) forces, being new troops, most of them under fire for the first time, must have fallen into a disastrous panic." This might well have been true if the projected attack could have been engineered faultlessly. At the time of writing Beauregard seems momentarily to have forgotten that his own men were in like condition and it is more than likely that his lieutenants would have been quite incapable, in these too early days, of performing such a delicate and wide-ranging pincer movement.

About the time that Johnston began his march towards Ashby's Gap in the Blue Ridge, Union troops were beginning to feel out Beauregard's positions covering Michell's and Blackburn's Fords. As will be seen, this was especially productive on the Union side, in that its strong rebuttal was the root cause of McDowell's subsequent flanking movement, but what is interesting is its effect on Beauregard's planning. Aware that Johnston and Holmes were now rushing to his aid, and elated by the success of his troops in their first Battle of Bull Run, he resolved to take the offensive if McDowell did not immediately renew the fight. McDowell did not. He held back until Sunday by which time Beauregard had perfected his arrangements; his left would hold the probable Union advance in that quarter while the right flank brigades would circle northwards in a terrible echelon of fire upon the Union camps in and behind Centreville. Orders for the commencement of this scythe-like manoeuvre were sent to Early on the extreme right at about 0530 hours that eventful Sunday morning but they did not reach him and the plan was eventually abandoned. In the light of what actually occurred during the day, it is interesting to speculate on the possible consequences both for McDowell and for the Southern generals, had both the actual Union and the projected Confederate right-flanking moves occurred simultaneously.

While Beauregard's thoughts alternated between sweeping aggression and barren withdrawal, his classmate across the river was equally beset by difficulties. A general plan to remove the Army of the Potomac from Manassas by threatening the railroad in its rear originated in McDowell's office during June. Congress approved and, though Scott had reservations believing that the Mississippi should provide the route to success, McDowell went ahead.

McDowell's intelligence service at this time seems to have been fairly good. At any rate his estimate that the Confederates numbered 25,000 at Manassas was fairly accurate, and he thought that they might collect another 10,000 once things began to move. These would not be Johnston's men, as McDowell's plan depended on the fact that Patterson must hold, "amuse", attack, or do anything possible to keep Johnston in the Valley. In the belief that Patterson was doing just that, McDowell set off, after inevitable delays and with the utmost caution, along the roads to Fairfax Court House.

At this time, the Northern General had only a vague idea that he might turn his enemy's flank. Wisely he did not commit himself to a detailed prognosis until he had gained a clearer idea of the area and of Beauregard's dispositions. Perhaps, secretly, he hoped that Beauregard would withdraw; though this would not have helped much because many of the Union ninety-day volunteer regiments were due for release in a few days time.

Once at Centreville with his leading Division, McDowell busied himself with reconnaissance. This took two forms — firstly, the usual method of sending scouting patrols to right and left to see where the emeny's flanks lay and where they might be turned and, secondly, the despatch of a small force along the direct road towards Manassas in an effort to assess the strength of the enemy's centre, and also to "keep up the impression that we are moving on Manassas." This task of reconnaissance in force was given to Tyler, the commander of the First Division, who used the major part of Richardson's Brigade together with eight guns in what developed into a noisy and unauthorised drive against the few Confederates who had remained on the north side of Bull Run and a lively little fire-fight across the normally peaceful waters of Blackburn's Ford. It was during this episode that Beauregard lost his dinner when an accurate Union shell burst into his McLean House Headquarters.

Meanwhile, McDowell himself was scouring the countryside opposite Beauregard's right only to find it unsuitable for his purpose. The combined effect of his inability to find a left flank route and the depression which had resulted from his rebuff at Blackburn's Ford was to convince him that he must manoeuvre the Confederates out from behind Bull Run and that he must do it by a right flank march. Thus events conspired to thrust a plan into his lap, and, whether or not the military expert now pronounces that it was a good plan, McDowell could do very little about it at the time, except sit down and work out the details.

The main detail had to be the route to be used by his flanking columns. The "perfect practibility" of this route was decided upon, after a reconnaissance on 19th July by Major John Barnard and Captain Woodbury of the Engineers, who, with the young Governor of Rhode Island and a troop of cavalry, rode north from the Warrenton Pike along the Cub Run Valley. They discovered a private road and they believed that the troops would be able to follow this eventually to Sudley Springs — though they did not themselves travel as far as Sudley because of enemy patrols in the area. These same enemy patrols foiled a night approach which Barnard attempted in company with some woodsmen who were found in one of the Michigan Regiments. McDowell accepted Barnard's reports and planned accordingly. Hunter and Heintzelman were to envelop the enemy's left flank and then drive it away from the Warrenton Pike to open the passage across the Stone Bridge for Tyler's men, who, in the meantime, were to "feint the main attack" against it. Richardson's brigade, some regiments of which were already sadly familiar with the area, was to make a "false attack" on Blackburn's Ford. Though he preferred an early start, General McDowell, not so long ago an artillery major, deferred, surprisingly to Colonels Hunter and Heintzelman, allowing their arguments for a single march to over-ride his own predilection for a programme which would have included a Saturday evening deployment along the roads followed by a restful breakfast *en route* and a resumption of the march at dawn on Sunday morning.

There was one defective link in McDowell's chain of thought. That link was his trust in Patterson, or rather Patterson's own intelligence service which gave the old general the idea that

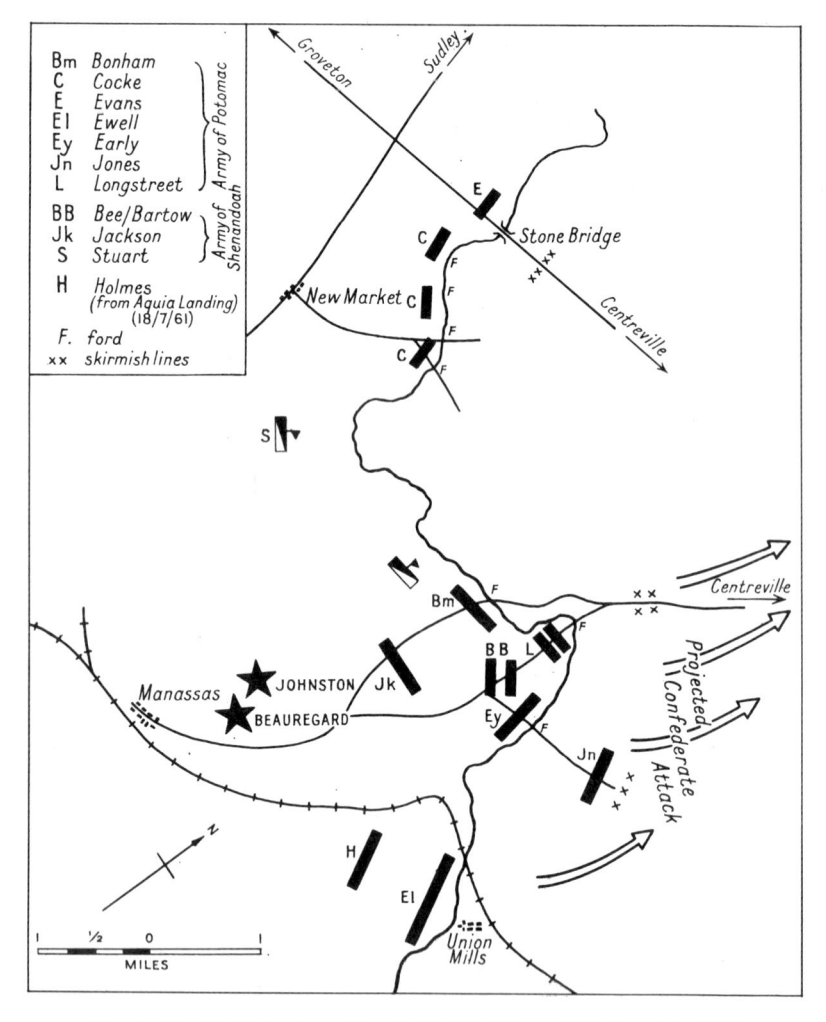

Map 6. The Confederate position behind Bull Run, 20th-21st July 1861

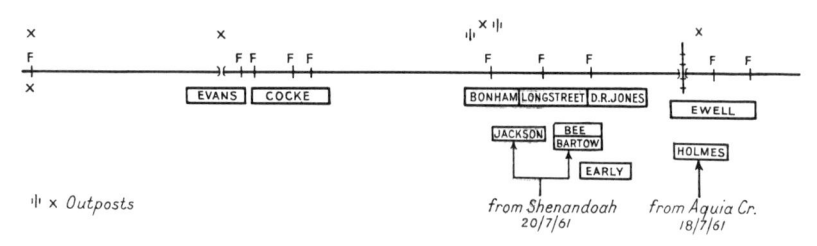

Map 7. The Confederate position behind Bull Run (diagrammatic)

Johnston had 26,000 men in the Shenandoah Valley. It has been shewn[1] that Patterson's intelligence men were at fault rather than Patterson himself, though, if the realistic estimates of one of them, D. H. Strother, had been accepted, then it is possible that Patterson might have engaged Johnston too closely to have allowed the Confederate move to Manassas. Thus, McDowell was robbed of his only real chance of success by the action of self-opinionated and muddle-minded officers in an army operating many miles away. The fact that he compounded his mistake by delaying his movement for two days, thus allowing Johnston and Holmes to combine with Beauregard, seems to be neither here nor there when seen in this light.

A very weary Johnston, sleepless since Wednesday morning, arrived at Manassas on Saturday, 20th July. By the small hours of Sunday morning he had slept and was ready to look over Beauregard's plan. In general he seems to have approved the idea of an attack against Centreville but in detail he was disturbed by the unequal distribution of the troops along the Bull Run line. While he asserts in one place that the only plan that Beauregard offered had been the move via Aldie, he is at some pains elsewhere in the same article[2] to shew that Beauregard's brigade dispositions were unlikely to secure success in a move against Centreville. In any case, the initial movements of the Union attack soon caused Johnston to weaken Beauregard's projected offensive when he ordered that Bee and Jackson be moved over to the left. "These with Cocke's Brigade, then near the Turnpike, would necessarily receive the threatened attack."

From this point onwards we must agree with Johnston that "the battle fought was on McDowell's plan, not General Beauregard's."

We cannot be sure of McDowell's feelings when, on Sunday morning, his three-month volunteers rubbed the cramp from their limbs and, spitting out the bad taste of too little sleep, began to move along the Turnpike. There was that niggling rumour that Johnston was already at Manassas. There were the newspapermen and civilian know-it-alls and their ignorant ladies thronging his camps like the members of some genteel fan-club of the future, about to watch the once-only, never-to-be-forgotten performance of their idol. There was all this business of rations and cooking and supply-trains.[3] There was old General Scott back in Washington, the team-manager who was expecting so much from his first-string. Most of all there was the Blackburn's Ford episode, now two days old, still depressing and underlining the fact that this polyglot army of farm boys and factory hands was hardly ready for war. Still, he had told the politicians all the way up to Lincoln himself that he did not think his men ready, but in a democracy the politicians listen to the people and the people wanted to fight. The ninety-day soldiers were to perform a nine-day wonder and then they could all go home. Perhaps — but at that moment they were facing the other way, and as the boys plodded and stopped, plodded and stopped on the road (which was not really a road) to Sudley, so Irwin McDowell's thoughts must have plodded wearily back over the events of the past few days.

Whatever his thoughts, he was brought sharply back to the business in hand when the sound of his first guns opening against the Confederate positions at dawn rolled across the plateau tops. At this time the flanking column was still short of Sudley. Tyler, with his 1st Division (less Richardson's Brigade) had had plenty of time to move up to the slopes leading down to the Stone Bridge, so much time in fact, that he seems to have forgotten that the divisions waiting behind him could not move across Cub Run until he had moved out of their way. Now Tyler was opening his demonstration on time, but partly because of his laggard movement a couple of hours earlier, the men he was supporting were nowhere near where they should have been. As it turned out, McDowell might have had more success if he had accompanied Tyler instead of waiting at the point where Hunter had turned right off the Pike, and then, with the dawn, galloping off in the wake of Hunter's column. However, during the first hours of daylight he was able, eventually, to get this column across the Sudley Fords between 0900 and 0930 hours, some two or three hours later than he had hoped.

At this juncture we can make a brief survey of the battleground as the sun, rising from beyond Union Mills floods the valley with light and reveals the dun-coloured dust clouds drifting up above Cub Run and the glistening steel and brass of the troops crossing the streams at Sudley. Here Burnside's Rhode Islanders, New Hampshiremen and men of New York pause to drink and splash while Porter's New York Militiamen grumble to the Regulars as they wait their turn to cross the river. Behind these, raising the dust are the three brigades of Heintzelman's division.

Tyler's skirmishers are beginning to move down towards Bull Run and the Stone Bridge. Behind them Sherman, Keyes and, south of the Pike, Schenck, stand with their men — four New York Regiments, three Connecticut, one Maine and three more from the Mid-West. Meanwhile "Fighting Dick" Richardson is in position along the Centreville-Manassas roads where they fall towards Mitchell's and Blackburn's Fords. Behind, in Centreville, Miles's well-rested 5th Division form a reserve with much of

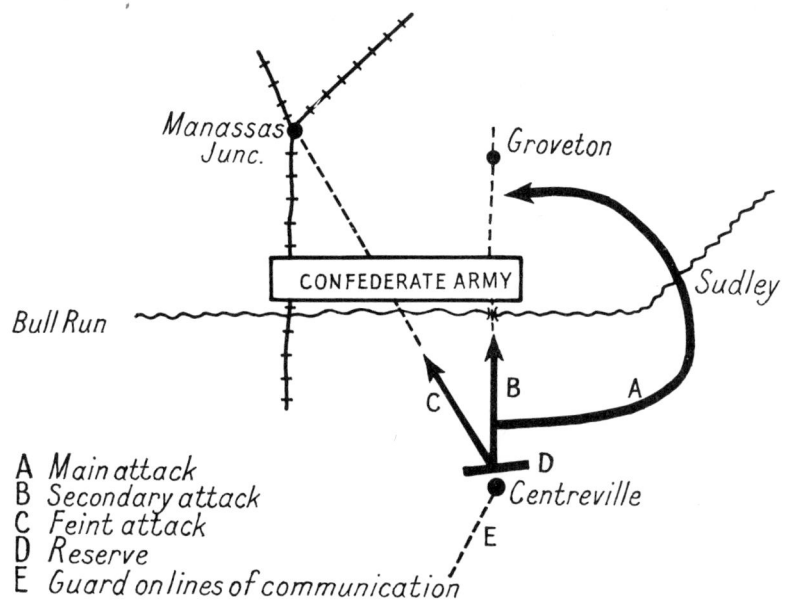

A Main attack
B Secondary attack
C Feint attack
D Reserve
E Guard on lines of communication

Map 8. McDowell's plan

the Union artillery. Runyon's reserve division, the 4th, of New Jersey regiments is far to the rear.

On the Confederate side of the river there is a great deal of movement. Weapons glint as columns move through field and thicket, raising dust which adds to that raised by the furiously galloping horses of couriers. The Union Mills sector however, is fairly peaceful and there Ewell gazes stolidly down on the wrecked bridge. Further upstream, D. R. Jones, Longstreet and Bonham with some troops now pushed across onto the left bank watch Richardson's men opposite. Behind them, on the roads leading over towards Portici and the Stone Bridge, Bee Bartow and Hampton with Imboden's guns, followed closely by Jackson, are racing to reinforce the threatened left. Here a thinly stretched line of Cocke's Virginians watch the river especially in front of the Lewis and Island Fords. On their left, four companies of the 4th South Carolina and a depleted battery cover the bridge. The bulk of Evans's command, which had been given the task of defending the bridge, has moved away westwards and is taking up a position in the vicinity of the Matthews house to counter the threat developing against his original flank, from the direction of Sudley. Far to the west, Kirby Smith's Brigade is entraining at Piedmont Station from whence it will be carried towards Manassas Junction.

CHAPTER IV

The Blow Falls

HAD "Shanks" Evans, even after seeing the dust-clouds rising above the trees on his left front and receiving confirmatory reports both from the small Confederate outposts at Sudley and from the Chief Signal Officer, decided that McDowell's flanking movement was none of his concern, the main Union attack must certainly have caused more trouble than it did. This dapper captain[1] of Confederate cavalry was promoted colonel soon after the battle, largely because of the initiative and gallantry he displayed in turning to trip Hunter's leading brigades as they emerged from Sudley hollow up on to Matthews spur.

The Union column was made up of five brigades. Burnside led, followed by Porter, Franklin and Willcox. Howard, with Heinzelman's third brigade, was held at the turn-off near Cub Run by McDowell himself and for reasons best known to himself, until dawn when they were allowed to follow in the now well-lighted wake of their comrades. As they made their twelve mile (19 km) way, many of these men from Maine and Vermont must have wondered anxiously if they would ever return to their friendlier Northern pine woods, especially when they heard the crackling strains of the Burnside-Evans duet accompanied by the booming of the rifled batteries back down Bull Run.

Ambrose Everett Burnside, six feet tall, firearms manufacturer and Colonel of the 1st Rhode Island Volunteers and said by Grant, much later, not to be a suitable man to command an army, was very busy at about 1000 hours this particular morning with one regiment. He was shepherding his boys into a line of battle and was perhaps disturbed that his Divisional Commander, Hunter, should be so busy organising his regiment's skirmish line when he ought properly to be making arrangements for Porter to bring the other brigade up in support. Burnside's leading regiment, the 2nd Rhode Island, had a battery of rifled thirteen-pounders attached and it was while putting these into place that Hunter was badly wounded. Porter, who was with

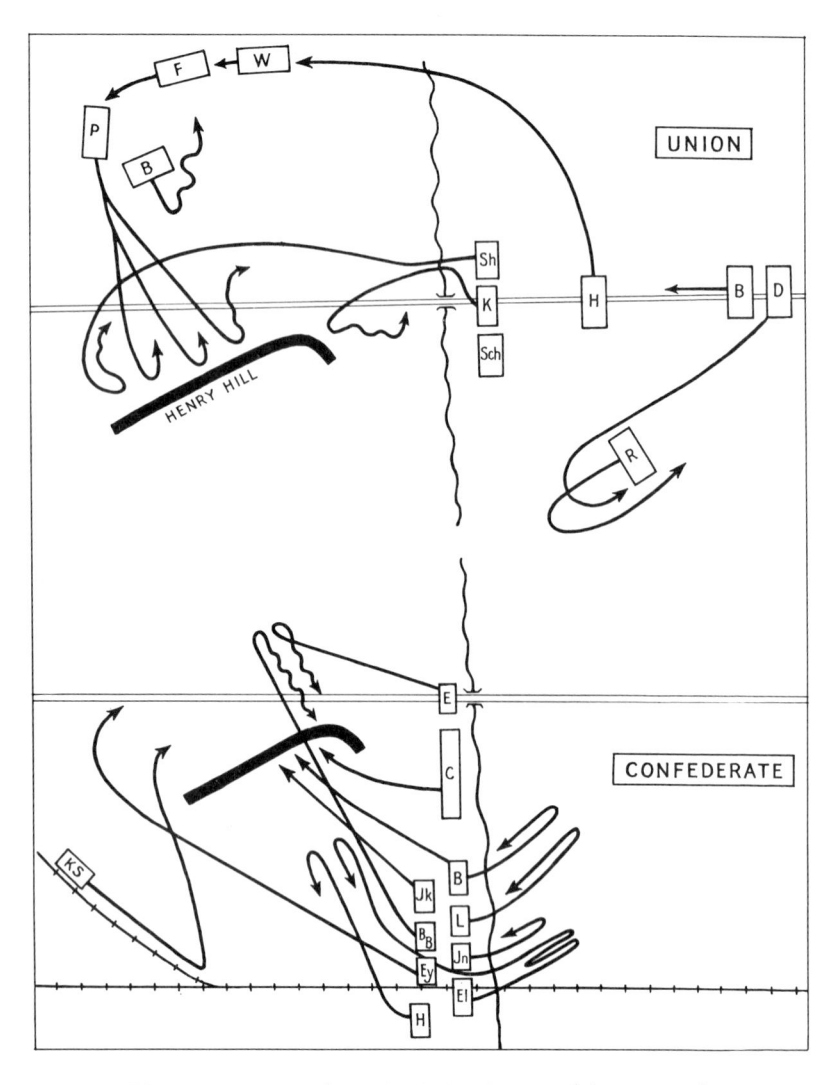

Map 9. Movements of brigades during the battle (diagrammatic)

the other brigade of the division, took command and Burnside was left to get on with the task of removing Evans's few companies.

The task was not easy. Evans, with a six-pounder gun-howitzer at each end of his thin line, had placed his small command on either side of a small copse on the Matthews land just to the east of the Sudley-Manassas Pike. Burnside's line came out of the fringe of a wooded area which screened much of the Sudley Road from the Confederate view.

Twice the Union volunteers charged in their efforts to prise the stubborn Louisiana Tigers and the South Carolinians from their hastily chosen position. Only the Rhode Islanders made the first attack but, after re-forming and recovering from the first shock of battle, they were joined by the rest of their brigade. Four regiments now supported by eight guns[2] yelled and screamed as they made their advance across a stubbly field against eleven Southern companies and two very hot little guns. The Southerners still held and Burnside's force was driven back into the trees where it was joined by the Regular Army battalion of Major George Sykes and by Griffin's battery of U.S. Artillery from Porter's Brigade. The resolution of Evans's small command, impressive still after more than a century, certainly impressed their attackers, for, while Andrew Porter sweated to deploy his rear regiments, Burnside hunkered down in the relative safety of his wood and continued to pour fire towards the smoke-puffs which marked the position of his ambushers.

It is surprising that Evans's stand on the Matthews spur never gained the same prominence in histories of the War as did Jackson's subsequent effort on the Henry Hill. Jackson's exploits as Lee's "right arm", his brilliant Valley campaign, his eccentricities and the solid nickname he gained during the Bull Run fight may all have something to do with the aura that surrounds the almost legendary incident. Evans, on the other hand, did not figure prominently in Confederate records after Bull Run except as the leader of the small Confederate force engaged at Balls Bluff in October, 1861. A South Carolinian and a dragoon with some Indian-fighting experience, he commanded an independent brigade which saw wide service during 1862. Then, in 1863, came two courts-martial, one for drunkenness and one for failing to obey orders; he was acquitted of both charges. After the War he became Head of an Alabama school. The stand that he inspired during this July mid-morning was truly his "hour of glory" and it seems a pity that the Horatian effort of his small command did not embed itself more deeply into the American imagination.

There is too, a touch of irony in the fact that it was Burnside who came up against this stout defence. Almost throughout his military career, it seems, his chance of making a name for himself as a general — rather than as a tonsorial model — was blighted by Southern tenacity. At Antietam, his division was badly mauled in crossing the "Burnside Bridge". At Fredericksburg his whole Army suffered as the result of his pig-headed efforts to batter a way through to Richmond. Then, in 1864, came the "stupendous failure" of the Petersburg Mine Assault. It was as though this, his first action, was to be the pattern for his whole career.

Despite the obvious heroism of his now well-tried group, Evans knew that he could not hold back all of the 13,000 men who had marched past Sudley that morning. The Louisiana Tigers were already wavering; their leader, Major Chatham Wheat, at thirty-five a veteran of the U.S. Army in Mexico, of the Mexican Army and of Garibaldi's English Volunteers, had been hit in both lungs, and though he asserted that he did not yet feel like dying, he had to hand over command of his boisterous, baggy-trousered Tigers[3]. But they were not the same without Wheat to direct their energies.

A messenger from fellow-Carolinian Bee urged Evans to fall back across Young's Branch and onto the crest of the Henry Hill. Evans, who had been given the task of defending the Warrenton Pike, did not like the idea of abandoning it. He sent back to Bee a return invitation, intimating that together they might stem the Union tide. General Bee had hurried his and Colonel Bartow's brigade of Johnston's Shenandoah Army across from the reserve position where they had been catching up on lost sleep. Seeing the advantages of the Henry Hill, he had deployed his regiments together with Imboden's Staunton battery along the crest of this feature, facing north-west. From there they had a grand-stand view of the fight which Evans was conducting on the opposite side of the valley. Soon, Imboden's red-shirted college boys were joining in that fight as they plied rammer and sponge in an effort to disconcert Ricketts's artillerymen who had unlimbered near the Matthews House.

Beauregard tells how Bee, "generously yielding his own better judgment to Evans's persistence", marched his infantry across the valley and "threw them into action." Five Confederate regiments, Evans's depleted command and a couple of companies of the 11th Mississippi now faced the combined might of the 2nd and 3rd Divisions of McDowell's Army.

They could not hold them for long. Although all of Heintzelman's Division were not yet present to enter this competition, they were not far away. By now, McDowell was calling for them to hurry forward. At the same time he sent messengers with orders to Tyler to press forward against the Stone Bridge. Tyler received this directive at about 1100 hours but another hour went by before he passed the order on to his third brigade which was commanded by Sherman. Meanwhile, the Confederates were beginning to give way before the ever-lengthening line of Union regiments, and it was soon evident that Bee's judgement had been better than that of Evans. As Heintzelman's regiments puffed up from Sudley they took over the pursuit, while Burnside's men, out of ammunition, filed to the rear. It seems then that it was Sykes's regular battalion, Reynolds's U.S. Marines, the balance of Porter's brigade — who were largely New York Militiamen — and the three regiments of Franklin's brigade (Heintzelman's Division) together with Griffin's and Ricketts's batteries, the latter having unlimbered on the western side of the Sudley Pike, who finally broke the Southern grip and began to push forward down the slope to Young's Branch. In this they were eventually joined by Sherman's men who had been led across Bull Run upstream of the Stone Bridge.

These regiments of Sherman's brigade (Tyler's Division) the 13th, 69th and 79th New York, and Peck's grey clad 2nd Wisconsin[4] were later to take a prominent part in the battle. It is significant that they sustained casualties to the extent of 23% of the total Union dead and 19% of the total Union killed and wounded. There has been some controversy however, about the part that Sherman played in the initial success against the Confederates north of Young's Branch. From the times given by various sources for Sherman's crossing of Bull Run and for the beginning of the Bee-Bartow-Evans retreat, it would appear that the Confederates began to fall back at about 1130 hours, but that they did not then fly in panic. During the withdrawal,

Sherman's men appeared to their right across the Carter fields, though by this time the now straggling grey lines must have been re-crossing Young's Branch. J. B. Fry, who was McDowell's Chief of Staff, writes that "Sherman reported to McDowell on the field and joined in the pursuit of Bee's forces across the valley of Young's Branch. Keyes's brigade followed . . . but without uniting with the other forces on the field, made a feeble advance upon the slope of the plateau toward the Robinson house."

Since the Red House Ford (sometimes called the Poplar Ford) lies about one and a half miles (2½ km) north of the Warrenton Turnpike, in the bend where Bull Run swings southwards towards the Stone Bridge and while it is another mile and a half from this ford to the area where Bee was engaged, it seems unlikely that Sherman's men, who had been facing the Stone Bridge, and who did not receive orders to cross until about noon, could have taken much part in the harassment of the Confederate retreat which began at about 1130 hours. On the other hand, if Sherman crossed the stream by a farm ford which lay only five hundred yards upstream from the Stone Bridge, and which lay in front of his position — then he could have engaged Bee's men at about 1230 hours, after a short advance across Van Pelt's fields. The story goes that it was Major Wheat of the Tigers who had revealed the position of the ford by which Sherman later crossed the Run, when early on that fateful morning he had impetuously yelled defiance at Union men who had interrupted his scouting mission across the river. It seems more likely that Wheat would have been scouting in front of the position he was ordered to defend (Stone Bridge and the farm ford) rather than riding more than a mile upstream. Imboden writes that Sherman "had crossed Bull Run *not far* above the Stone Bridge at a farm ford", and while it is admitted that "not far" could mean one and a half miles, it seems more likely that, given the dimensions of the battlefield, the Virginian gunner is referring to a distance of five hundred yards.[5]

From his position near the Henry farmstead Imboden's men saw Bee's regiments retiring down to the marshy meadows which formed the Young's Branch valley. For half an hour after this they saw no Confederate troops, but they were able to watch the renewed advance of the Union flanking column as it moved down to the vicinity of the Stone House. There appears to have been no lull in the battle, however, for by now, out to the new Confederate right flank, Hampton's Legion had rushed up to make a stand along the Turnpike by the Robinson Farm. Keyes, who followed Sherman, fell foul of these six hundred South Carolinians whose determination was reflected in their casualty figure for that day — 120 men!

However, the commands of Hampton and Imboden were the only Confederate units which stood in any semblance of order to face the Union pursuit just after noon — and both were heavily engaged, as the dishevelled groups of Bee's men filtered through to the rear. Filling the Sudley Road and the Matthews fields came the New Yorkers of Porter, Sherman and Willcox, and other regiments who made up their brigades; the men of Wisconsin and Michigan and the Massachusetts and Minnesota regiments of Franklin's brigade. These and the searching shells of Ricketts's, Griffin's and Arnold's batteries hounded their retreating enemy into a confusion of despair, while McDowell thought, too soon, that he had crushed a rebellion. His tired eyes and tidy mind told him, however, that he must reform his own Army before pressing his advantage further. He saw, as Bee had seen, that could he once occupy the Henry House Hill, then he could present Manassas and the line to Richmond to his President and a grateful Nation.

Ricketts and Griffin, who had divided their explosive attentions between Bee's infantry and Imboden's Staunton battery, were ordered to limber up and race to the Henry House, Imboden having fallen back from his first position and out of sight of the Union troops. During the lull which ensued, the Union brigades were reorganised more or less along the line of the Warrenton Pike, the bulk of the force standing in the area of the Stone House crossroads.

By this time the Confederate command had divined McDowell's purpose, though until Richardson's men were reported to be felling trees along the slopes above Mitchell's and Blackburn's Fords, Johnston was loath to send too many men to his extreme left. Up to this time, about 1100 hours, only Bee, with Bartow's brigade, Hampton and Jackson had been sent to Evans's aid. Jackson's brigade arrived last and took up a position along the top fringe of a large pine thicket which clothed the south-east slopes of the Henry Hill, so that his line fronted the crest of the hill across which the Union brigades were expected to advance. Cocke's brigade, facing eastwards across the river covered the right rear of Jackson's line while J. E. B. Stuart's two hundred cavalrymen protected the left flank by coming up into the oak woods around the eastern flanks of Bald Hill. This was the core of the Confederate defence at about half-past noon, but, like a magnet, it was attracting the scattered particles of Bee's force. Bee himself was mortally wounded shortly after having pointed out the resemblance of

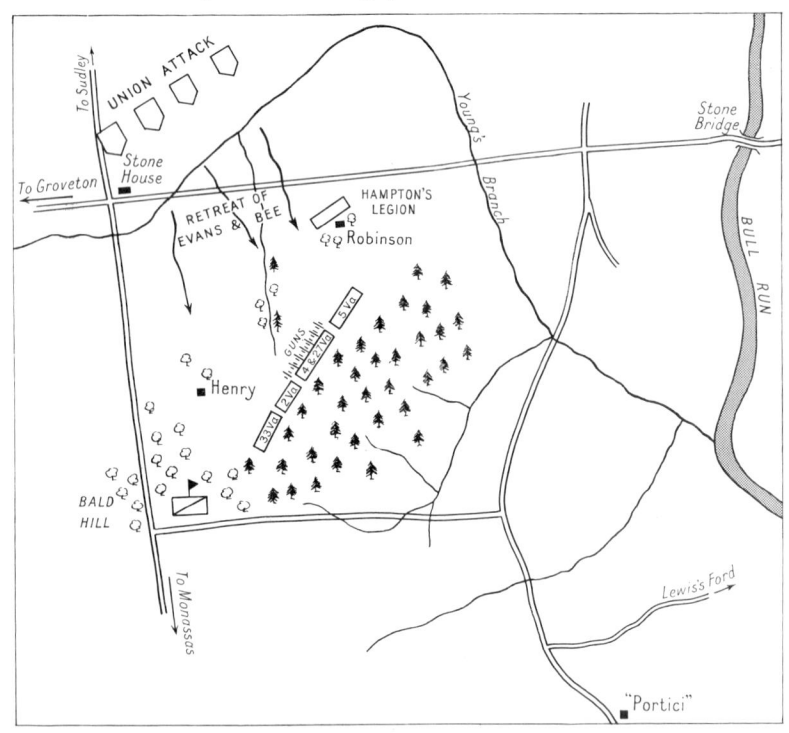

Map 10. Jackson's "Stone Wall"

Jackson's line to a stone wall, but his idea took root and soon more and more stragglers saw fit to "rally behind the Virginians". Three companies of the 49th Virginia tramped up from Cocke's brigade behind "Extra Billy" Smith, a former Governor of their State, and soon Brockenbrough's Rockbridge, and Heaton's, Leesburg battery came up to relieve the Staunton guns which were now totally without ammunition. Eventually twenty-six guns joined the lines which Beauregard and Johnston were now busily arranging, after the latter had sent urgent orders for Early, Holmes and Ewell to come to Jackson's support. Now the chaotic disorder began to resolve itself into lines of men, as officers spurred across the uneven ground, yelling and shouting orders taking their cue from Beauregard, Johnston and Jackson. Eventually, according to Johnston's arithmetic, "we had 9 regiments of infantry, 5 batteries and 300 cavalry of the Army of the Shenandoah, and about 2 regiments and a half of infantry, 6 companies of cavalry and 6 field-pieces of the Army of the Potomac, holding at bay 3 divisions of the enemy." So they gathered, except for the dead, the wounded and the skulkers, around Jackson's Virginian wall — the 7th Georgia, Fisher's 6th North Carolina, the 4th Alabama — all that could be gathered in along the wooded fringe of the Henry fields.

The re-formation of battle lines proceeded in like manner in the sedge-grass pastures of the marshy Young's Branch valley and along stretches of the Turnpike. Already the 11th New York Fire Zouaves of Willcox and the 14th N.Y. (Brooklyn) of Porter had been sent plunging up the slope to protect the Union batteries unlimbering by the Henry House to face Jackson's almost hidden line. As other regiments formed, they too followed up the hill towards the rising crescendo of noise which capped it.

It was at this point that McDowell and his lieutenants made two grave errors. The blame for the first seems to rest upon Tyler's shoulders. This officer had accompanied Keyes when his first brigade followed Sherman's third brigade across Bull Run leaving Schenck and the second brigade in front of the Stone Bridge. As we have seen, Keyes came up against Hampton's Legion at the Robinson holding. When Hampton withdrew to Jackson's line, the Federals slanted left following the valley of Young's Branch. By this time — about 1400 hours — the Bridge was cleared and it seems that Tyler might have brought Schenck across and, with the united strength of two brigades, fallen upon the right of Jackson's line which was hardly protected by Cocke's force still facing across the Lewis and Ball's Fords. To Fry in 1884, McDowell, referring to Tyler, wrote: "If there is anything clearer to me than anything else with reference to our operations in that campaign (1st Bull Run), it is that if we had had another commander for our right we should have had a complete and brilliant success." We leave the reader to decide.

McDowell's second error may have had as much to do with the quality of his brigade commanders and the tired newness of his troops as with the brevity of his own apprenticeship in Army command. It was that he failed to assault the new Confederate line with all his available regiments in a concerted drive that might have dislodged his enemy. It is probably true to say that, by now, his brigade organisation, except for that of Sherman, was so disrupted by the shock of battle that the regiment became the basic tactical unit. Not all commanders were paying attention to their proper duties. For example, Heintzelman, a divisional commander, was seen leading the 11th New York Regiment to its position in support of the Artillery when he should have been overseeing the deployment of his two brigades and the bringing forward of Howard's regiments.

Of course it is possible that McDowell considered that the Confederates had crumbled, in which case, after a brief pause, his continued advance was to be a pursuit rather than an advance against a formed enemy. He had no way of knowing that the flight of Bee's men had been stemmed and he must have been hoping that his feint against Blackburn's and Mitchell's Fords was having the effect of holding the bulk of the Confederates in that area. On the other hand he must have realised by then that most of the troops who so far had stood in his way were from the Shenandoah, so that he was fighting two armies and not one.

Whatever his thoughts, McDowell decided to pursue the attack. As we have seen, regiments were re-formed and despatched up the slope. Sherman led his regiments directly along the Sudley-Manassas Turnpike while Michigan and Minnesota regiments from Heintzelman's Division followed the more direct gulleys up towards the noise on the hill crest.

CHAPTER V

The Confederate Counter

THE Confederate Generals' decision to abandon all thought of an attack on Centreville and to concentrate their efforts upon repelling the main Union assault was made none too soon. Ordering the troops who were to remain along the river between Mitchell's Ford and Union Mills to make strong demonstrations against Richardson's men, Johnston and Beauregard hurried towards the clamour which had grown so ominously in the Stone Bridge area. Once on the Henry Hill they were quick to endorse the decision already made by Jackson, and, as we have seen, they busied themselves in extending the Virginian's *stone wall.* In the emergency Cocke, holding the fords immediately below Stone Bridge, was asked to provide some men, and it was about the time when the 49th and 8th Virginia Regiments came breathlessly up the hill that Johnston galloped back to Portici to superintend the shunting of reinforcements up to Beauregard who had sensibly taken command of the threatened sector leaving the Shenandoah general free to look after the whole Confederate force. Beauregard was familiar with the area and, despite later acrimony on the subject, it is fairly obvious that once Johnston had arrived at Manassas he had taken the burden of overall command from Beauregard's shoulders while accepting the latter's wider knowledge of the field of operations. To allow his subordinate to take charge in the position of greatest danger was not only a form of military etiquette but downright commonsense.

Beauregard was an ideal commander for the situation which had now developed, but to Jackson must go the credit for the initiation of and, by example, for the strength of the defensive line which Beauregard perfected and then used to defeat the eager Union attack. While Hampton's Legion held off Keyes's brigade, Jackson, gathering Imboden's battery under his wing, disposed his regiments along the curving edge of pines just below the crest of the spur. In the centre, behind the artillery with its five guns and three shells, he placed the 4th and 27th Virginia with the 2nd and 33rd on their left. On their right the 5th Virginia extended to the right towards the Robinson farm (Map 10, page 34). This was the *stone wall* which Bee indicated to his retiring men and, as it happened, placed it in the pages of history.

All of these regiments came from the eighteen counties which lie in the Shenandoah Valley; counties which had first been settled during the second quarter of the eighteenth century by immigrants from the Rhenish Palatine in Germany and by Presbyterians from Ulster. Both peoples had a tradition of rugged vigour, splendid individualism and unswerving devotion to "good causes". Fighting Indians, Frenchmen and the British only served to ensure that these prime frontier traits were passed on intact to their progeny who, now stamped with the imprint of Jackson's own discipline, showed them all in their steady bearing as they awaited the holocaust. Loath to leave the rich cornlands and verdant meadows surrounding their quiet hamlet homes, especially since Patterson might even now be rampaging freely through the Valley, these five regiments, the First Brigade of the Army of the Shenandoah, now stood apparently the sole buttress of the States' Rights cause. Bee caught the moment — or to be more accurate, there were enough men within earshot to catch his words, so that months later, when the Confederacy had time to catch its breath, Jackson's brigade was officially honoured with the now almost legendary nickname.

Bee called it a wall but the Brigade acted more as a net so that many knots of dejected men who had fought under Bee and who were now straggling across the crest of the hill could not but be caught both literally and metaphorically by its crescent. Officers behind the spur were soon able to collect many of those who had escaped round its tip or along the Sudley-Manassas Road and lead them up to the crowded ridge where they could once more rally on their standards. Here, across from the oaks which hide the Sudley Road, the reforming ranks of Gartrell's Georgians and Faulkner's Mississippians; there, pulling back from the Robinson House, the badly mauled men who follow Wade Hampton, and coming up to them, the fresh 8th Virginians of Cocke's brigade whom we left climbing from the Run. Shells from Arnold's Union Battery, still across on the Matthews slope, crash among the young pines of the Confederate position with sickening regularity, while Jackson rides along the line telling the men that all is well. Some of the shells fall amongst the crowding men so that screams of agony add a counterpoint to the chorussing exhortations of colonels and majors. But while Beauregard, one horse already killed beneath him, can gallop along the crest and while Jackson behaves as if he were on Church Parade — where indeed he would have been had he commanded the army — the men stand firm, the grey wall growing perceptibly stronger with each passing minute.

General Fry wrote that, "the several struggles for the plateau were at close quarters and gallant on both sides". In any such fight it is difficult to verify and correlate all the incidents which are later reported. The participants lose all sense of time and details often loom so large upon the tensed minds of the reporters as to prohibit a balanced view. Bearing this in mind, we have taken Beauregard's description of the Henry House fighting as a basis for our own account. Though it is sometimes difficult to reconcile with other accounts, we feel that the Confederate general's deposition is as reliable as any and it gives a good idea of the varying fortunes of the contestants in this series of purely frontal attacks, charges and counter-charges. In the windless afternoon air the dust and smoke only added to the confusion. Fortunately our task is not as difficult as that faced by the historian who wishes to describe, for example, the fog-bound field of Inkerman — but it is difficult enough.

Naturally, McDowell made the first move. Not waiting to form true lines of assault, a couple of regiments were gathered in by Heintzelman and Major Barry, the chief gunner, to be hurried forward with Ricketts's and Griffin's batteries. Heintzelman with the 14th New York and Barry with the Fire Zouaves (11th N.Y.) accompanied the guns to a position near the Henry House, now battered by the previous shelling, and with its owner lying stricken inside. Meanwhile, McDowell, ordering advances to continue towards the crest and along the Sudley Road, set his army an example by riding up to the Henry House so that he might better ascertain the extent of the Confederate retreat. As he peered from a bedroom window his surprise at finding the now steady line just beyond the crest must have matched that of the Fire Zouaves who, upon taking position near the Union guns were immediately charged by Stuart's Virginia Cavalry. This force had been stationed in the oak

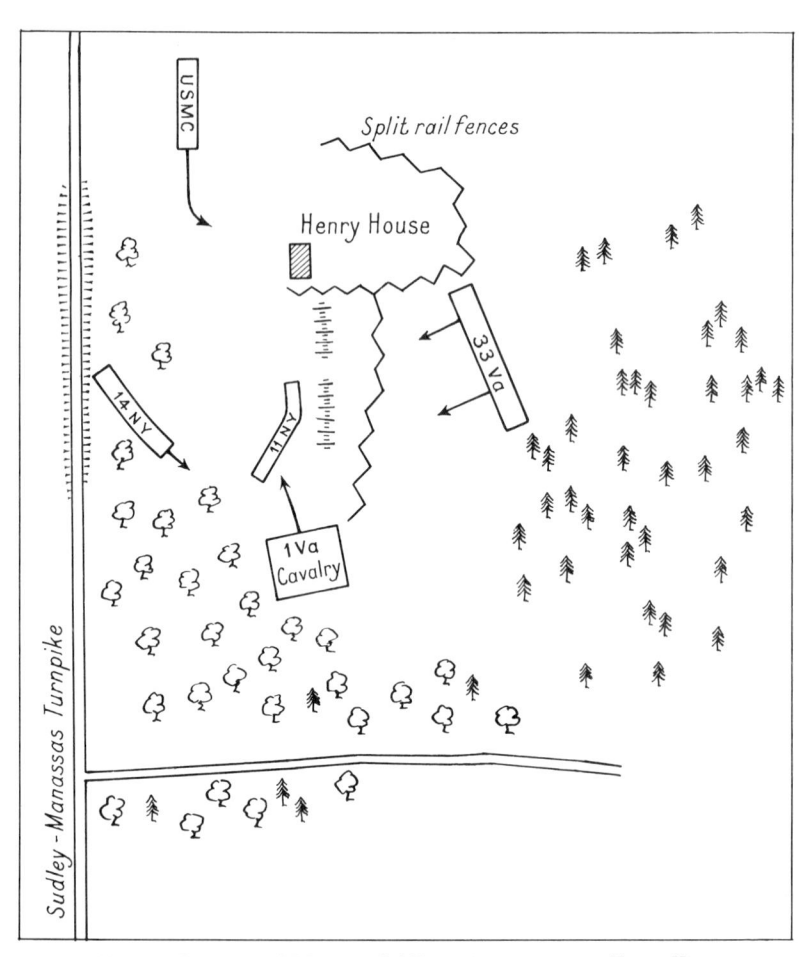

Map 11. Positions of Ricketts, Griffin and supports near Henry House

thickets between the Sudley Pike and the Georgians at the western end of Beauregard's line (see Map 10, page 34). Yelling and slashing, the cavalrymen on their black horses charged through the broken ranks but failed to dislodge either the red-fezzed firemen or the sweating gunners. Coolly the New Yorkers emptied their rifles at their attackers who swung round to the left and crossed the slopes back to the Sudley Pike. What did cause the Zouaves to come to grief was the close approach of Jackson's 33rd Virginians clad in blue tunics and with the "Stars and Bars" hanging limp in the still, smoke-hung air. Barry failed

40

to recognise them for what they were and their telling volley at less than a hundred yards poured into gunners, horses and infantry supports alike.

The advance of the 33rd Virginia indicates that in the Henry House sector of the conflict, which lay in front of the centre-left of Beauregard's line of battle, the Union advance was so close to his own lines that he was in danger of being completely outflanked. To combat this he initiated a charge on his right, which, spreading along the full length of his regiments, bull-dozed the Northerners completely "off the whole of the open surface of the plateau". The Union guns, which had been recaptured from the 33rd Virginia, now fell into Southern hands a second time.

After a short respite, McDowell now made a second major attempt to capture the hill. Once more regiments acted more or less independently and, though Howard's brigade had now come up to support it, the thrust became, in essence, a series of finger jabs. Nevertheless, the Henry and Robinson houses were retaken, although Sherman's report of his own regiments' efforts against the Confederate left flank tells how first his grey-clad Wisconsin regiment "fell into confusion", then how the 79th New York (Highlanders) "finally broke" and how Corcoran's 69th N.Y. (Irish) "held the ground for some time; but finally fell back in disorder". One wonders what might have happened had he been allowed by McDowell's staff-officer, who ordered this manner of attack, to attack with all three regiments at once.[1]

"The conflict now became very severe for the final possession of this position, which was the key to victory ... I knew that I was safe if I could hold out till the arrival of reinforcements, which was but a matter of time ... It was now between half-past 2 and 3 o'clock". Thus wrote Beauregard, who adds that he was prepared to allow his force to be "surrounded on all sides, until assistance should come". We believe that he may be a little out in his reckoning of the time in this instance, and would put the second Union thrust nearer to 1400 hours, though this has, in fact, very little bearing upon the course of the struggle.

Whatever the time, Beauregard did not allow McDowell to gain too firm a foothold along the crest of the hill. Believing attack to be the best form of defence he advanced his entire line and the separate regiments in blue once more tumbled back down to the Young's Branch meadows. By this time, however, so many Union troops had joined McDowell's line that it now stretched beyond the Stone House and was edging into the south-west angle of the roads. While the Confederate attack had been very successful on the right, where the 18th Virginia, Cocke's brigade, had been thrown forward with Hampton's Legion, the Sudley Road end of the line was still threatened by Sykes's regulars and Howard's New England regiments.

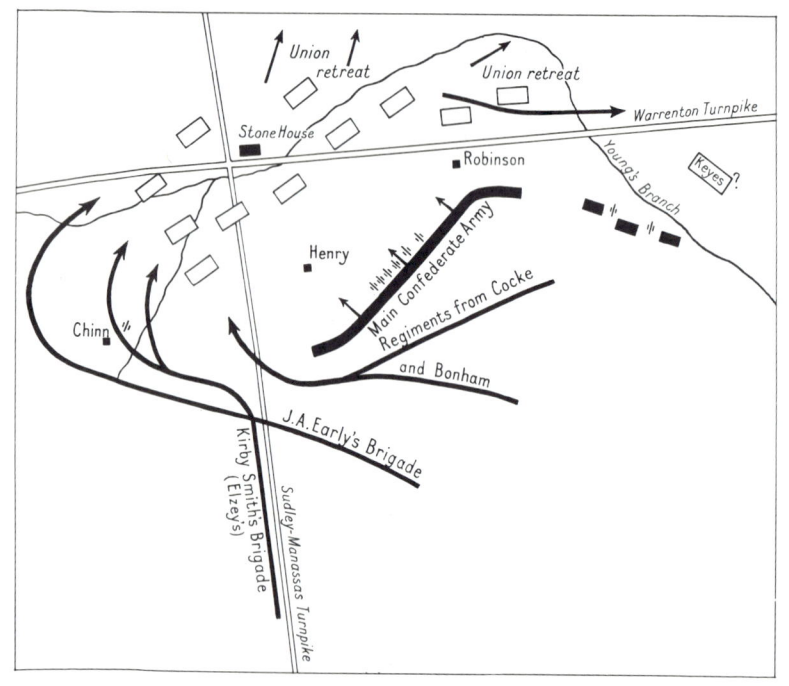

Map 12. The Confederate flank attack

It was at this juncture that Johnston's able management began to pay dividends; two South Carolina regiments of Bonham's command, along with the Alexandria battery, were directed along the Sudley Road and quickly went to work to disrupt the Union right. In this they were joined by the 28th Virginia, another of Cocke's regiments, which managed to capture Colonel Willcox, who was directing the 1st Michigan in this sector. Following up this attack there now appeared the long-awaited last brigade from the Shenandoah. Kirby Smith, at the head of two more Virginian regiments, (one of which was learning soldiering under Colonel A. P. Hill), the 3rd Tennessee, the 1st Maryland and Beckham's Battery, was directed to take station on the left of Bonham's South Carolina reinforcements. Although Smith, because of an early wound, had to hand over command to Elzey, these men, who had arrived at Manassas about the time that Jackson was building his Wall, soon began to prove to McDowell that his efforts were wasted. If he was not convinced immediately, then the subsequent arrival of Colonel Jubal Early's four regiments on Elzey's left soon confirmed his worst fears and, more important, the fears of all but a handful of his troops. The sturdy resistance along the Henry Hill crest now coupled with the obvious superiority of the Confederate reserves was enough. A final attack by Beauregard made absolutely certain of the ownership of the Henry House Hill top and the possession of a grandstand view of the Northerners' misfortune.

Misfortune indeed, but no panic. One of the most significant facts which appears in more than one description of the Union withdrawal is that a substantial number of Northerners escaped the wrath of a triumphant enemy by retreating along the Warrenton Turnpike and across the Stone Bridge. Beauregard wrote: "Major Sykes's Regulars, aided by Sherman's brigade, made a steady and handsome withdrawal, protecting the rear of the routed forces, and enabling many to escape by the Stone Bridge". Further significance we think, for we have seen that both Sherman and Sykes had fought on the right of the Union line yet now they were helping their comrades escape by the left flank. While there can be little surprise that Keyes, for example must leave the field at this point, we must assume that the Confederate counter-attack to clear the hill of Union troops was not pressed home in the vicinity of the Robinson house. In fact, the attack is more likely to have been a steady and slow advance rather than an exhilarating forward sweep like that of the Allies at Waterloo. It is fairly certain that Sykes and Sherman had not moved across the front of the Confederate line at an earlier stage for Fry tells us that at about 1630 hours he ordered Arnold's battery, who were then unlimbered "about where Evans had taken position in the morning", to join Sykes's battalion and Palmer's cavalry to cover the rear. This implies that, at that time, Sykes at least was still west of the bridge while, at the same time, a movement towards the bridge from the Matthews Spur was quite feasible.[2]

It is evident that the Confederates did not get the bit between their teeth and that Jackson's Virginians and the regiments which supported them were content in their fatigue and exultation to stop and watch Elzey and Early, together with J. E. B. Stuart who had joined in the attack against the Union right, shepherd McDowell's army off the field. There were fresh Union troops across Bull Run, of course. At some indeterminate time, and on his own initiative, Fry sent orders to Dixon Miles, who held the 5th Division in reserve at Centreville, to move his two brigades up to the Stone Bridge. Colonel Louis Blenker, who had Miles's first brigade, received his orders to move forward at about 1600 hours. "The 8th (New York Volunteers) Regiment took position one and a half miles south (*sic*) of Centreville, on both sides of the road leading to Bull Run", he reports. "The 29th (New York) Regiment stood half a mile behind the 8th, *en echiquier* by companies. The Garibaldi Guard stood as reserve in line behind the 29th Regiment. The retreat of great numbers of flying soldiers continued till 9 o'clock in the evening..."

It will be remembered that when Tyler, with Keyes, followed Sherman across Bull Run, he left Schenck's brigade on the Centreville side and one might have expected to find mention of this brigade's activities during the Union retreat but the spotlight remains upon Sykes, Sherman and Blenker. Further, it is rather remarkable that the latter moved only one and a half miles (2½ km) out along the road towards the Stone Bridge, which means that he did not reach even the Cub Run bridge. He was alone, of course, because Miles's other brigade was supporting Richardson's "false attack".[3]

Most of the troops on the left of McDowell's line quitted the battlefield along the Sudley Road and through the Sudley fords. It has been computed that men of the 2nd and 3rd Divisions who used this escape-route must have marched twenty-five miles (40 km) from Centreville to the Stone House and back, to which they added a further twenty miles (32 km) by the time they had reached the Potomac. Forty-five miles and five or six hours of hot summer battle and all in thirty-six hours!

At the same time the Confederate infantrymen were happy to rest and as they allowed the joys of relaxation to pervade their bodies, they were content to leave pursuit to the cavalry. "Jeb" Stuart followed the Sudley Road and two squadrons of the 30th Virginia under Colonel Radford set off from Portici and crossed the river at Ball's Ford with a view to harassing their enemies on the Turnpike. It may have been these who "molested" Blenker's men between 2100 hours and midnight, after most of the Union men had passed through his position.

Things had not been entirely quiet in the Blackburn's Ford area and lower down the river. We have seen that Richardson's assumption of a defensive pose on the slopes above the main crossings had allowed Johnston to send brigades and regiments to help Bee and Jackson. Before this time the Southern generals had been expecting to see the development of an attack against Centreville by Ewell, D. R. Jones and Longstreet. Although this never materialised, Ewell did in fact cross the river at about 1000 hours after seeing Jones's copy of Beauregard's orders. However he was recalled when Beauregard began to appreciate the strength of McDowell's attack on the Confederate left. During the afternoon Johnston issued an order for Ewell to advance across the river again to demonstrate against the Union forces around Centreville. Also at about 1400 hours, Johnston received a report that a U.S. army (*sic*) was approaching from the north-west, so he sent orders to Bonham, Longstreet and Jones to remain south of the river and to be ready to move. Ewell's skirmishers were already engaging Richardson's troops when he received a second recall with a supplementary order to "move by the most direct route at once and as rapidly as possible, for the Lewis house". Nearer the head-quarters he halted and, though he asked permission to join in the pursuit, his request was refused.

A little later in the afternoon, Johnston received reports of a large Union force crossing Bull Run at McLean's Ford. He recalled Beauregard, who was enjoying a hopeful move across Lewis's Ford to intercept the retreating men on the Turnpike, and the Creole general mounted some infantrymen behind his cavalrymen and set off to eliminate the new danger, leaving orders for Ewell and Holmes to follow. No more glory for one day though, "Some nervous person" had suffered an attack of "jitters" when he saw General Jones recrossing from the north bank.

Apparently it was not only Jones who was returning to the Southern lines. At 1640 hours Johnston, hearing of the Union collapse sent orders to Bonham and Longstreet to march by the quickest possible route to intercept McDowell's retreat along the Warrenton Turnpike. How close these men approached to the Pike we do not know, but surprisingly they did not interfere because they found "so little appearance of rout in those troops as to make the execution of (their) instructions seem impracticable". Even more surprisingly, they then turned round and returned to their camps. It is most likely that "those troops" were, in fact, members of Richardson's brigades. By order of Miles, the two brigades which had been pushed out towards Mitchell's and Blackburn's Fords — Richardson's fourth brigade of the 1st Division and Davies's second brigade of the 5th Division — were pulled slowly back towards Centreville. The road they used was, on the map, the quickest possible route by which Bonham and Longstreet might advance and it is not unlikely that Richardson did his best to persuade the Confederates that though it might be a possible route, it was certainly not the quickest.

First Bull Run was a very mobile battle. Almost everyone seemed to be called on to do a lot of marching or riding, especially on the Confederate side. Of all the brigades, Holmes's seems to have been regrettably slow. While it is true that his morning reserve position behind Ewell, who watched the Union Mills crossings, placed him furthest from the Henry Hill — except for Ewell himself — he received his orders to go swiftly to the threatened left at about 1100 hours. Jubal Early, between McLean's Ford and Manassas, made the slightly shorter journey in sufficient time to arrive in the area of the Chinn House by shortly before 1600 hours. Kirby Smith, detraining at Manassas Station at noon, reached the field even before Early, yet Holmes had "just arrived" in the vicinity of Portici "when the retreat began", according to Johnston, who was able to employ his men in countering a Union "demonstration on the rear of our right". In passing, it is interesting to note that Holmes displayed an unfortunate timidity a year later when with more verve he might have seriously affected McClellan's retreat to Malvern Hill during the Peninsula Campaign. He was fifty-seven years old when he marched his two regiments up from Aquia Creek to strengthen Beauregard, and his later record shews that he felt the strain of high command to be too much for him. However, he had been at West Point with Jefferson Davis in the late twenties, and appears to have allowed his President friend's insistence to over-ride his own sensibilities. In an ill-considered action at Helena in Arkansas during the summer of 1863, however, he proved his point and was then sent to finish the War as the commander of North Carolina's reserves.

Holmes's apparent lack of vigour is thrown into greater relief by the pugnacity of all the Southern commanders who were involved in the main Bull Run action. Evans's tenacity shades into the capability of Bee and Bartow, both killed in action, while the imperturbable Jackson and the excitable Stuart, so similar in character yet so different in mien, were examples for all who fought near them. And then there was Beauregard himself who, like Stuart, had the power to inspire the innate fighting spirit of the Southerners. To these must be added Kershaw, of later fame, the impetuous Jubal Early and equally impetuous A. P. Hill, Barksdale, fearless Kemper, Hampton, Elzey and so on.

However, the reason for the success of the Confederate counter-attack is not to be found solely in the character of the Southern leaders. There were many equally brave men in McDowell's army, and, though success finally eluded them, the battle might well have gone the other way.

CHAPTER VI

The Triumphant South

LONG after McDowell's weary soldiers had dragged themselves into Alexandria, and long after the final resolution of the War itself, Beauregard saw the outcome of the Bull Run battle as "the gradual result of the operation of many forces, both of opposing design and actual collision, modified more or less by the falls of chance." We shall be looking at some of these "falls of chance" in the next Chapter while the opposing designs of each side was examined in Chapter III. It seems appropriate that now, having tried to give a fair picture of the "actual collision" in Chapters IV and V, we should attempt to evaluate Beauregard's conclusion that, regardless of minor accidents, this first major battle of the War was bound to result in a Confederate victory.

It was not an overwhelming victory because militarily it had little effect on the overall strategic situation which had prevailed before McDowell's advance. Blenker and Richardson covered the pathetic race back to Alexandria and, after a majority of his troops had decided that they were going home and that they intended to travel the first stage as far as the Potomac that night, their general gave up his ideas of making a stand in Centreville. Accordingly the Confederates once again advanced to Fairfax and soon their picquets were able to look down on the Alexandria lines almost as though nothing had happened. Spiritually, of course, the effects of the battle were very far-reaching as any good history of the War points out, and it is because much of the character of the subsequent fighting might have been very different if McDowell had been successful, that it seems worthwhile to look for the "many forces" which Beauregard believed had led inevitably to McDowell's defeat.

In his *History of the Confederate War,* Eggleston makes something of the fact that the Southern recruit was accustomed to the use of firearms and the rigours of outdoor life, whereas the Union men "were accustomed to nothing of the sort." He further argues that the Virginians especially, coming from "that nearly roadless state", were peculiarly suited to the cavalry arm. The authors have read this sort of thing time and again in subsequent histories and have wondered if Eggleston or some other early twentieth century scholar set a fashion for such theses. The "roadless state" argument is seen to be a poor one when we consider the conditions of transport prevailing in almost any American State at this time, except perhaps those of southern New England and the heavily peopled parts of New York, New Jersey and Pennsylvania. And while it is true to say that the Virginian cavalrymen at this time were mainly recruited from the leisured, horse-owning class, it is hardly correct to assert that no-one in the Union Army had been a civilian gentleman with time on his hands, a lack of roads in his area, and a horse or two in his stables.

A major defect in the "customary use of firearms" argument comes to light in an examination of the recruit potential of the Southern States. It is not true that the Confederate regiments were packed with plantation owners. Most Southerners could not afford to own slaves. They were small farmers and many were poor, small farmers. Many were used to handling firearms, certainly, but hardly more so than the woodsmen of Michigan and Maine and the farmers of Wisconsin, Illinois or even Connecticut and Pennsylvania. If the Confederates had any advantage in this context it lay in the fact that many Union regiments were recruited from small milling towns as in Massachusetts, from coal mining towns as in Pennsylvania, and from the foundries, warehouses, building sites, packing plants and docks of such cities as New York, Boston and Philadelphia. There may be something in the theory that these men were at a disadvantage because of being totally unused to the arts of weaponry, though they may well have compensated for this by being more amenable to training in disciplined team-work than the more individualistic farmer. It is difficult to assess, but easy to imagine, the benefits to morale of military service in company with friends, workmates and neighbours. The high morale of the "Pals Battalions" in the British volunteer army of 1914 might be remembered in this connection. Of course, on both sides communities sent their young volunteers to war in companies and batteries where almost every man from Colonel to drummer-boy came from the same county or town. We have already mentioned Jackson's Shenandoah Valley regiments, and there is a good example in the New York Fire Zouaves. It would be an idle exercise to try to determine which side may have benefited most from this system and our conclusion is that the armies were probably equally balanced in this respect.

One point of significance is that in this battle, as in so much of the bitter fighting of the following years, the Union troops were invaders while almost every man following the "Stars and Bars" felt that he was defending his family, virtually in his own back yard. Of the forty-five infantry regiments ready to contest the Bull Run crossings, seventeen were Virginian.[1]

The military historian can seldom explain the outcome of a major battle in terms of numbers employed by each side. Sometimes, as at Malvern Hill, it is a matter of the number of big guns. More often it is a matter of training, efficiency and discipline. In our battle, these factors differed to an exceptional degree between some of the various units involved, but, generally speaking, there seems to have been little to choose between the average Union and the average Confederate regiment. Neither had spent long periods on the drill square, for example. McDowell's men had been brigaded only a few days before the battle, though most of them had completed several weeks of military service.

The first new regiment mustered on the 29th April was the 1st Minnesota[2] so that, apart from Militia training and apart from the battalion of Regulars, all of the Union men at Bull Run can be said to have had three months of training or less[3]. With good officers this might have been enough, especially if the regular soldiers had been distributed as N.C.O.s among the raw youths whose only qualifications under the Militia Acts of 1792 and 1795 were that they were "between eighteen and forty-five years of age and in physical strength and vigor."[4] Scott said that the Regular Army men should not be scattered among the volunteer regiments and had his way. Even so, the amateur soldiers who had been trained by amateur instructors did not disgrace themselves. Whether or not the Union troops might have done better had Scott allowed Lincoln to mix the whisky and the water is debatable. We would merely point out to the reader that an appraisal of the generally good service performed by the very young British National Servicemen of the 1950s, often in trying conditions and after only a few weeks of instruction, leads one to believe that Scott was wrong.

Whatever the case, the regimental organisation seems to have stood up under the Bull Run test until about 1600 hours when the Army began to degenerate into a mob of individuals. Indeed, at the regimental level, it was the Southerners who first shewed signs of strain, when Bee's command fell back from the Mathews Hill. One wonders what might have been the outcome if Jackson had not chosen quite such a strong position on which to make a stand.

It was the brigade and divisional organization which was at fault on the Union side. It is generally accepted that of all the Northern units engaged in heavy fighting, Sherman's brigade was outstanding in its steadiness, yet Sherman had been given hardly two weeks in which to organise it. If we judge from his later career that he was the best of the Union leaders on the field, then the point need hardly be laboured more.

Was it then that the Confederate command structure was superior to that of the Union? Jackson's Stonewall Brigade was formed and effectively hammered into shape with Bible and Drill-Manual by their superlative Colonel from April 28th onwards. On the other hand, Bee, Bartow and Kirby Smith did not organise their commands until 24th May, though even this gave them a longer period in which to do their work than was enjoyed by Sherman and his colleagues. An additional point in the Shenandoah Army's favour is that it had had the advantage of exercising itself in the face of an enemy force and had even succeeded in exchanging a few blows with it.[5] Of the other commanders whose troops took part in the main struggle around the Henry Hill, Bonham had been involved with his brigade at Vienna on 7th June while Cocke had been training his troops throughout most of May and June. From this it must be assumed that the Confederates probably had a slight advantage. This is most obvious in the case of Jackson's command, perhaps, but the authors doubt if this was in any way decisive.

The staff-work in both armies was poor. Because of Confederate failings in this respect, the projected right flank drive by Ewell, Longstreet and Jones did not materialise — perhaps fortunately for the Union side. McDowell's failure to achieve a concerted forward movement during the afternoon and to obtain positive support from that part of his army which was not engaged both point to similar deficiencies. The McDowell we see peering from Judith Henry's bedroom window was McDowell the Major of Artillery rather than McDowell the Brigadier-General. This tendency to perform a subordinate's duties is observed in many of the senior Union officers at Bull Run. We have seen, for instance, Hunter shot down while organising skirmishers when he should have been directing his brigades. It is possible that they behaved in this manner because they felt that they could not trust their juniors. On the other hand, staff-work apart, the intelligent way in which the two Confederate generals divided their duties gave the Southern side an overwhelming advantage in that it was thus enabled to execute a tactical manoeuvre — the outflanking of the Union main attack — almost with the finesse of a talented veteran force. With Beauregard holding down the almost captive enemy, Johnston was able to direct what turned out to be almost a death-blow. From the numbers involved, we can fairly safely assume that, even if his men had decided to stay and fight, McDowell would still have been forced to retire by the advent of Elzey and Early who, in short time, would have been reinforced by Holmes and Ewell.

There remains to be considered the question of strategy and tactics. In the following Chapter we shall explore in detail a number of considerations in this sphere, but in our present search for an explanation of the Confederates' success, we must mention what we consider to be the over-riding general feature of the battle. It is that the defender has the odds in his favour and that he has an inordinate chance of success if his forces are equal or superior in number to those of the attacker. If there was any irony in First Bull Run — or indeed, if at any time that the battle was taking place, there was any doubt about the ultimate outcome — it lay in the fact that the Confederates were forced to fight in a defensive position which was not of their own initial choosing. What happened here was to be repeated two years later at Gettysburg when it was the Union army which fought successfully to defend an off-the-cuff position chosen in haste. It happened twice again to Johnston at New Hope Church and Kenesaw Mountain in the Atlanta campaign, though Sherman then more or less side-stepped so that Johnston gained no real advantage from the strong positions he had been "forced" to occupy.

Of course, the object of inducing one's opponent to move to a new position is to relieve him of all the advantages he has built into his original, prepared position. A classic example of the application of such a move is afforded by Wolfe at Quebec in 1759. The French were persuaded to move out of a virtually unassailable position to meet the British troops on equal terms in a position of the latter's choosing. In the case of Bull Run, the Confederates were forced to move from a strong position behind the river crossings to meet McDowell's thrust which had already crossed the river to their flank. The difference between the fortunes of the French at Quebec and the Confederates in Virginia lies in the simple fact that Montcalm was unlikely to be able to find a suitable defensible position on the Plains of Abraham whereas Jackson found an eminently suitable, even Wellingtonian, position on the Henry Hill. It is to be noted that Bee had found the same position but had unwisely and even unwillingly abandoned it with inevitable results. Jackson earned his nickname because it implied that, like a wall, he would not move backwards, but he really *deserved* it at the time it was bestowed because, like a wall, he would not move *forward!*

The other difference between Montcalm and Johnston is that the latter, unfortunately for McDowell, had extra troops to send to the new position, so that he was lucky in not having to weaken his (or Beauregard's) original first-choice positions. If the Army of the Shenandoah had not been moved to Manassas, then the Confederates must have been forced to move. Up to this point McDowell's inducement had been almost first-class. But when Jackson was fortunate enough to discover a new defensive position then, unless McDowell could think of a variation on the right flanking theme, the value of his inducement at once disappeared. While no-one would argue that Jackson's new position was as strong as, say, Longstreet's or Jones's position at the fords, it was certainly better than that chosen by Evans on the Matthews spur. Then when McDowell found it beyond his ability to do more than hurl his regiments against Jackson's line, the battle might be seen as the forerunner of many a later Civil War fight in that it took on the character of a battle of attrition. It was merely a matter of who could stay longer on the top of the Henry Hill, and in this contest the Confederates won by a short head — mainly because they were there first and so they became the defenders. McDowell seems to have been quite prepared to continue his dogged attempts with all the lack of sublety of a Western Front General in 1916, but the arrival of outflanking forces under Elzey and Early caused the fight to revert to its previous mobile character, by which time the weary Union men had had enough.

We do not propose to enter the lists in the old and barren argument concerning the failure of Johnston and Beauregard to follow the shattered Union forces into Alexandria and to capture Washington. While many believed that this should have been the main result of the battle, we believe, with Johnston, that it was one of the major results of the battle that the Confederates were unable to do so. He wrote that, "our army was more disorganised by victory than that of the United States by defeat." As Wellington said of Waterloo, it had been a close run thing. Perhaps we can shew in Chapter VII that Beauregard's determinist verdict was further from the mark than Johnston's matter of fact pronouncement.

CHAPTER VII

The Falls of Chance

ALL students of Military History will agree that the greatest battle ever fought was the *Battle of If!* Perhaps the military historian is more tempted than his colleagues in other branches of the subject to consider how different things might have been if certain accidents had not occurred or if certain decisions had not been made. On the other hand, there are cogent arguments to sustain him in rejecting these temptations, but this book is offered principally to the Wargamer who, in the pursuit of his hobby, is not only free of purely academic restrictions but is often more interested in pursuing what might have been rather than in the slavish re-creation of what actually happened.

In the preceding Chapter we emphasised the general tactical development of McDowell's success in inducing Johnston to move troops to an unprepared position, Jackson's success in adapting this position for defence and McDowell's subsequent failure to counter with a new move to dislodge Jackson before being himself outflanked by Elzey and Early. It seems appropriate that we should now attempt an assessment of this development by examining briefly a few of the possibilities open to the prime mover.[1]

Our first "if" must concern the combination of the two Confederate Armies. We have pointed out Patterson's lack of aggression in the Shenandoah Valley and, though K. P. Williams[2] has given the Pennsylvania veteran a fairly adequate absolution, the fact remains that but for events beyond the Blue Ridge, Beauregard might have been forced to face McDowell's 32,000 men with only 23,000 instead of the 35,000 actually available for the battle. Many have wondered if the hero of Sumter might still have held Manassas against such odds. We have shewn that his thoughts dithered between attack and retreat and yet, had he stayed to face McDowell's thrust by despatching, say, Bonham, Longstreet and Early to make a stand on the Henry Hill, he would have left three brigades (counting Holmes) to cover the lower crossings and would have placed thirteen regiments across McDowell's path. The regiments of Jackson, Bee and Bartow, and Smith numbered fourteen and of these Smith's four regiments, whose casualties totalled 27 men, were hardly engaged. Thus, with Evans's command and Hampton's Legion excluded from these figures, it would seem that McDowell's task would have been difficult even without Jackson's brigade to strengthen his enemy's determination.

McDowell's column had marched a long way during the eight hours before Burnside stumbled against Evans near the Matthews farm. Would it not have been better to send three divisions against the Stone Bridge? On a map shewing the fords and the Confederate dispositions this looks to be fairly easy and perhaps even obvious. But McDowell was not sure of his enemy's numbers, nor of how many were behind the river's various crossing places. The steep river banks made Bull Run a difficult obstacle to overcome, and the Northern Commander must have had little doubt that Beauregard could easily have moved more troops to this flank by the time his cumbersome brigades had made their purpose clear by deploying on the forward slopes overlooking the bridge itself. In any case, while he had engineer officers (used largely for scouting) he had neither specialist engineer troops nor bridging apparatus. On this count then, we cannot fault McDowell's plan, though its timing and the manner of its execution obviously left much to be desired.

Military experts are unanimous in their praise for Evans's display of initiative in taking the bulk of his force to face the Union flanking column. Lesser commanders might well have been afraid to leave the post of responsibility in front of the bridge and would have contented themselves by referring the matter to Cocke, who had overall command in this sector. The resulting ease with which Hunter and Heintzelman might have moved on towards the Henry Hill can be imagined. It will be seen that they might have advanced as easily if Evans had only moved onto the Henry Hill, a shift which would also have left the Stone Bridge open to Tyler. In the event, Evans delayed the head of the Union column while Tyler failed to grasp a golden opportunity to storm the four companies which had been left to confront him. In this matter, too, Hunter might usefully have ordered Burnside and then Porter to deploy more to their left so as, eventually, to make a stronger link with Tyler's men who, in any case, were expected to make the running in the drive towards Manassas. Such an extension would also mean that Evans would be outflanked and so forced to withdraw.

Despite Evans's brave action, McDowell's movements during the forenoon of 21st July were successful, though for various reasons they had been executed slowly. This run of good luck might have been prolonged further, perhaps, if he had chosen to manoeuvre on the flanks of the new Confederate line instead of trying to push it off the Henry Hill by frontal assault. Only one other alternative might be offered. Curbing what seems to have been a sudden and uncharacteristic bout of impatience, he might have insisted that Burnside rejoin the attack, that Porter, Franklin and Willcox reform their brigades and that Tyler's brigades — with or without Sherman — support a comprehensive assault by making adequate advances against the north-east end of Beauregard's line.

Of course, the brigade reorganisation would have given more time for Early and the others to bring up the Confederate reinforcements. On the other hand, there is reason to suppose that the Confederate line might have been so severely punished as to give possession of the Henry Hill to the Union men before these fresh supports could be flung against them. The roles of the contestants might thus have been reversed and the Southerners might have felt duty bound to expend their energies in an attempt to retake the position.

While considering this particular "if", mention must be made of McDowell's use of his cavalry. Palmer's eight companies of Regular horsemen came onto the field with Porter's brigade. The first hint that neither McDowell nor Porter had many ideas as to how to employ this force, comes when we note that it was not used to outflank Evans's men on the Matthews Spur. Later, when he might have been doing something to discomfort Beauregard's flanks or, possibly, to hinder Kirby Smith's approach, we can find no evidence that Palmer was ordered to do anything until he took a useful part in protecting the Union's retreating rear.

How Beauregard might have organised a new Confederate line if he had been pushed off the Henry Hill we have no way of knowing. Indeed, as intimated above, we wonder if, once in possession of the crest, McDowell would have tried to advance further towards Manassas before bringing up more troops. He was a cautious fighter and, already wary of a Confederate move to threaten his lifeline, he had strung Runyon's regiments all the way to within a few miles of Centreville and had deposited a further division in the village itself. The weary men who were with him, enlivened a little perhaps by success, but by now fully aware that war was not the picnic they had thought it might be, would probably have been more content to slink into the woodlands and wait to see what the "Rebs" would do next than to chase after them down the far slopes.

There remains the business of Beauregard's plan to attack the Union left. Johnston's forecast as to its effectiveness, as we have seen, differed widely from that of its originator. Throughout the War, the martial Louisianan urged that the small Southern armies should be used offensively and so it was natural for him to extoll the virtues of this his first brain-child long after the South had been defeated. Considering the relative strengths of the forces involved we would agree with Johnston that a frontal attack against Centreville would normally have failed, but we wonder if a movement directed against Fairfax instead of against the Union Army might have unhinged McDowell's own plans to such an extent as to cause him to retire northwards away from the direct approaches to Alexandria.

As things turned out, Beauregard might have won a more convincing victory if, instead of stacking so many regiments between Mitchell's Ford and Union Mills, he had planned to fight a defensive battle and distributed his troops more evenly along the river so that they were more evenly balanced. The allocation of more men to guard the Stone Bridge and the fords immediately below it would have saved a lot of shoe-leather and might have left Johnston's Shenandoah brigades free to move at will and even to cross Bull Run.

One final consideration. We find it hard to decide why Kirby Smith's brigade did not detrain at the point where the Railroad from the Valley crosses the Warrenton Turnpike at Gainesville. Such a move would have placed them on the Union flank much earlier and, perhaps more decisively.

One of the great problems when composing such a Chapter as this is that, having stated that a consideration is the final one, the minds of the authors go straight into top gear and produce another dozen. However, for reasons of space, we must leave further consideration to our reader who, with his private army, might explore more of the many options which present themselves so readily. We feel certain that if he undertakes to play out the "Battle of If" then that too will be decided, as was Bull Run, not only by strategic and tactical skill but also by the "Falls of Chance."

APPENDIX I

Notes on Chapters

Chapter I
1. Beauregard had commanded the force which had fired on Fort Sumter.

Chapter II
1. This description applies to the Centreville-Manassas area as it was in 1861. The present tense is used for the sake of clarity.
2. In the Battlefield Park Handbook, this feature is referred to as "Chinn's Ridge".
3. A glance at a contoured map shews the Henry House Hill to be, basically, a long spur which neatly fills the south-eastern angle between the crossing turnpikes. True, the bulk of the spur does appear to form a separate feature, especially when viewed from Bald Hill, primarily because a sub-tributary of Chinn's Branch almost cuts the "hill" completely from Bald Hill. The combined effect of the ravine so formed, the thickets which hide the actual surface across the neck of the spur, and the deep setting of the Sudley-Manassas Pike, is to give this part of the plateau the appearance of a separate hill. This effect is enhanced by the gentle upswelling of the hill's surface, the crown of which is now occupied by the Battlefield Park's Visitor's Center. Consequently the authors will retain the traditional name of "Henry Hill".
4. The commands of Early, Longstreet, Bee, Bartow and Jackson.
5. Before 1861, this area had been of too little importance to merit serious map-making so that both generals were totally dependent on reconnaissances. Perhaps this is the reason for the present variety of maps which purport to shew the main features of the battlefield area as it was in 1861. This is especially true of the road pattern. A comparison between the maps on p. 115 of Henderson's *Stonewall Jackson* and on p. 180 of Vol. 1 of *Battles and Leaders of the Civil War* and that on pp. 22-23 of the Manassas National Battlefield Park Handbook, shews three interpretations of the exact route of the road which passes

Portici for example. We tender an explanation to the effect that the area was covered by a substantial number of roads, tracks and bridle-paths, so that it was possible to move fairly easily in any desired general direction. Each map includes some of these trackways and omits those considered to be unimportant. Consequently, each of the maps must be considered reliable in itself and an amalgam of them all to be more comprehensive than any of them.

6. In view of the continuing process of metrication, each measurement will be followed by its metric equivalent. However, where the distance is given in yards it will not generally be followed by its equivalent as, for all practical purposes, the two are equal.

Chapter III
1. See pp. 82-85 of *Lincoln Finds a General* by K. P. Williams.
2. See the article, "Responsibilities For First Bull Run" in *Battles and Leaders*.
3. See *Lincoln Finds a General,* Footnote 88, Ch. 3, Vol. 1.

Chapter IV
1. There is some confusion as to Evans's rank at the battle. This could be due to his possession of a State rank higher than his CSA rank. We have taken that given in *A Civil War Dictionary*. This does not, however, resolve the problem.
2. The 71st N.Y. had two Dahlgren boat howitzers.
3. Wheat survived the battle and fought in the Valley Campaign. He was later killed at Gaines's Mill.
4. The 2nd Wisconsin wore grey uniforms and had enlisted their own Nurse, Anna Etheridge who was known as "Michigan Annie" or "Gentle Anna".
5. As further evidence that this was the Farm Ford near the Stone Bridge, we give the following from Sherman's Report: "The brigade was deployed in line along the skirt of the timber to the right of the Warrenton road ... (about 10 a.m.) we saw a rebel regiment leave its cover in our front and proceed in double-quick time on the road towards Sudley Springs". This must have been Evans's force and, had they been higher up stream — as they would need to be to fit in with the higher ford — then Sherman would not have been able to deduce their destination.

Chapter V
1. The men of Quinby's 13th N.Y. Regiment of rifles, Sherman's other regiment, were employed as skirmishers in the advance on the Henry Hill and "continued on up the hill, while the other 3

regiments changed direction by the right flank and followed the Sudley-Manassas road". Sherman's Report.

2. Both Sherman and Sykes formed irregular and hardly kept squares against cavalry and moved back to the river in these formations. Sherman's force recrossed at its crossing point earlier in the day.

3. We may presume that Blenker's "south of Centreville" really means south-west, since he says that his advance was made difficult by the retreating baggage wagons and "vast numbers of flying soldiers belonging to the various regiments". There were no retreating troops on the road from Mitchell's Ford because Richardson was engaging Holmes near the crossing at that time.

Chapter VI

1. On the Union side, even if one includes Runyon's uncommitted 4th Division which was composed of Jerseymen, there were fifteen N.Y. regiments out of a total of forty-nine. Of the remaining thirty-four a third came from New England. Only eight came from the Mid-West. In general, the cavalry and artillery were Regular U.S. units.

2. This Regiment lost more men than any other at Bull Run.

3. The USMC had less than three weeks. All other regiments — except fourteen — had sixty days.

4. Lincoln had to rely on Volunteers because 183 of the 198 Regular companies were needed on the western frontier where they were serving.

5. At Falling Waters, Bunker Hill and Charlestown.

Chapter VII

1. Hooker's inability to deal with Lee's similar movements at Chancellorsville in May, 1863, bears comparison with McDowell's paralysis. Hooker's plan to turn the Confederates' Fredericksburg defences behind the Rappahannock was very much like McDowell's plan for Bull Run. Lee turned to meet the Union flanking column and held it while Jackson outflanked the outflankers. In the face of this manoeuvre, Hooker withdrew across the river.

2. *Lincoln Finds a General,* Vol. 1, Ch. 3.

APPENDIX II

Orders of Battle

UNITED STATES FORCES
G. O. C. Brigadier-General I. McDowell.

1st Division; Brigadier-General D. Tyler.

1st Brigade; Keyes.
    2nd Maine
    1st Connecticut
    2nd Connecticut
    3rd Connecticut
Casualties; 19 killed, 50 wounded, 154 missing. Total 223.

2nd Brigade; Schenck.
    2nd New York Militia
    1st Ohio
    2nd Ohio (Carlisle Battery)
Casualties; 21 killed, 25 wounded, 52 missing. Total 98.

3rd Brigade; Sherman.
    13th New York
    2nd Wisconsin
    69th New York
    79th New York (Ayres Battery)
Casualties; 107 killed, 205 wounded, 293 missing. Total 605.

4th Brigade; Richardson.
    1st Massachusetts
    12th New York
    2nd Michigan
    3rd Michigan
    Edwards Battery
    Hunts Battery

2nd Division; Colonel Hunter

1st Brigade; Porter.
    8th New York Militia

    14th New York Militia
    27th New York
    Regular Battalion
    U.S.M.C. Battalion
    Palmer Cavalry (Griffin Battery)
Casualties; 86 killed, 177 wounded, 201 missing. Total 464.

2nd Brigade; Burnside.
    2nd New Hampshire
    1st Rhode Island
    2nd Rhode Island (Battery)
    71st New York (2 guns)
Casualties; 58 killed, 171 wounded, 134 missing. Total 363.

3rd Division; Colonel Heintzelman.

1st Brigade; Franklin.
    5th Massachusetts
    11th Massachusetts
    1st Minnesota (Ricketts Battery)
Casualties; 70 killed, 197 wounded, 92 missing. Total 359.

2nd Brigade; Willcox.
    11th New York
    38th New York
    1st Michigan
    4th Michigan (Arnold Battery)
Casualties; 65 killed, 177 wounded, 190 missing. Total 432.

3rd Brigade; Howard.
    3rd Maine
    4th Maine
    5th Maine
    2nd Vermont
Casualties; 27 killed, 100 wounded, 98 missing. Total 225.

4th Division; Brigadier-General Runyon.

This Division was not brigaded.
    1st New Jersey Militia
    2nd New Jersey Militia
    3rd New Jersey Militia
    4th New Jersey Militia
    1st New Jersey Volunteers
    2nd New Jersey Volunteers
    3rd New Jersey Volunteers
    41st New York

5th Division; Colonel Miles.

1st Brigade; Blenker.
    8th New York Volunteers
    29th New York
    39th New York
    27th Pennsylvania (Tidball Battery)
    Bookwood New York Battery
Casualties; 6 killed, 16 wounded, 96 missing. Total 118.

2nd Brigade; Davies.
    16th New York
    18th New York
    31st New York
    32nd New York
    (Greene Battery)
Casualties; 2 wounded, 1 missing. Total 3.

THE CONFEDERATE FORCES
G. O. C. in C. Brigadier-General J. Johnston.
Field Commander: Brigadier-General P. G. T. Beauregard.

The Army of the Potomac.

1st Brigade; Brigadier-General Bonham
    11th North Carolina
    2nd South Carolina
    3rd South Carolina
    7th South Carolina
    8th South Carolina
Casualties; 10 killed, 66 wounded. Total 76.

2nd Brigade; Brigadier-General Ewell.
    5th Alabama
    6th Alabama
    6th Louisiana

3rd Brigade; Brigadier-General Jones.
    17th Mississippi
    18th Mississippi
    5th South Carolina
Casualties; 13 killed, 62 wounded. Total 75.

4th Brigade; Brigadier-General Longstreet.
    5th North Carolina

    1st Virginia
    11th Virginia
    17th Virginia
Casualties; 2 killed, 12 wounded. Total 14.

5th Brigade; Colonel Cocke.
    8th Virginia
    18th Virginia
    19th Virginia
    28th Virginia
    49th Virginia (3 companies)
Casualties; 23 killed, 79 wounded, 2 missing. Total 104.

6th Brigade; Colonel Early.
    7th Louisiana
    13th Mississippi
    7th Virginia
    24th Virginia
Casualties; 12 killed, 67 wounded. Total 79.

Temporary Brigade; Captain/Colonel Evans.
    1st Louisiana Special Battalion
    4th South Carolina
    Terry's Cavalry
    Davidson's Battery

Reserve; Brigadier-General Holmes.
    1st Arkansas
    2nd Tennessee

Unattached;
    8th Louisiana
    Hampton's Legion
Casualties; 19 killed, 100 wounded, 2 missing. Total 121.

Cavalry;
    30th Virginia (Radford)
    Harrison's Battalion
    10 Independent Companies
Casualties; 5 killed, 8 wounded. Total 13.

Artillery;
    Bn. Washington Artillery La. (Walton)
    Alexandria Battery (Kemper)
    Latham's Battery (Latham)
    Loudoun Battery (Rogers)

Shields' Battery (Shields)
Casualties; 2 killed, 8 wounded. Total 10.

The Army of the Shenandoah.

1st Brigade; Brigadier-General Jackson
    2nd Virginia
    4th Virginia
    5th Virginia
    27th Virginia
    33rd Virginia
Casualties; 119 killed, 442 wounded. Total 561.

2nd Brigade; Colonel Bartow.
    7th Georgia
    8th Georgia
Casualties; 60 killed, 293 wounded. Total 353.

3rd Brigade; Brigadier-General Bee.
    4th Alabama
    2nd Mississippi
    11th Mississippi
    6th North Carolina (2 companies)
Casualties; 95 killed, 309 wounded, 1 missing. Total 405.

4th Brigade; Brigadier-General Smith.
    1st Maryland Battalion
    3rd Tennessee
    10th Virginia
    13th Virginia
Casualties; 8 killed, 19 wounded. Total 27.

Artillery:
    Imboden's Battery
    Stanard's Battery
    Pendleton's Battery
    Alburtis's Battery
    Beckham's Battery

Cavalry:
    1st Virginia (Stuart)

APPENDIX III

Arms

To understand the tactical manoeuvres on an American Civil War battlefield it is important to have a knowledge of the weaponry involved. It must never be forgotten that tactics are directly related to weapons and that a real development of the former is rarely achieved unless preceded or accompanied by a development of the latter. It is hoped that this Appendix will help to give the reader some knowledge of the basic weaponry of the period.

1. Infantry Small Arms.
The variety of arms used in the War Between the States was almost as great as that of the combatants' uniforms — both in appearance and practicability — so that an action was as likely to be decided by one side having superior weapons as it was by the tactics used. Most troops, certainly at Bull Run, had muzzle-loaders which could be — and often were — doubly, trebly or quadruply loaded following a misfire of the first load. After Gettysburg one rifle had twenty-six loads. Other men had seven shot magazine rifles which could be fired at least three times as quickly.

To decide which arms were carried by each unit at Bull Run would require research in far greater depth than would be compatible with a general work such as this. It is hoped, however, that the descriptions of various weapons given below will give some idea of the characteristics of the various small-arms used. Further information may be obtained from *Arms and Equipment of the Civil War* by Jack Coggins (Doubleday 1962) which is a most valuable reference book. It is profusely illustrated and contains a wealth of information on all aspects of its title. It also contains a very good bibliography.

Generally speaking, it may be said that the majority of infantrymen carried a single-shot, muzzle-loading, percussion lock, rifled-musket but that each side had a proportion of its forces armed with magazine weapons. Although smooth-bores were used, they may, for practical purposes, be ignored.

The Enfield Rifled Musket. Percussion lock. Muzzle loading. This British weapon was first generally used in the Crimean War. It had a calibre of ·577 inches and could be fired twice in one minute. It was sighted up to 900 yards but had been used at twelve-hundred yards with effect if not accuracy during the Indian Mutiny. It was a good, dependable weapon and was used both by North and South. The Confederates used rather more including a more elaborate officers' pattern known as the "Jeff Davis Enfield". It was also copied by several Southern gunsmiths.

The Springfield Rifled Musket. U.S. Model 1861. Percussion lock. Muzzle loading. This weapon had superseded the 1855 Model as the standard U.S. Rifle and almost 1,500,000 were used during the war. Similar in characteristics to the Enfield it had a slightly larger calibre of ·58 inches and weighed less than nine pounds. Its effective maximum range was five to six-hundred yards and it was deadly at less than three-hundred. Again, this was a dependable and serviceable weapon.

The Whitworth Rifled Musket. Percussion lock. Muzzle loading. This ·45 inch rifle had a barrel designed by Sir Joseph Whitworth, the precision-engineer. To prevent the ball over-riding the rifling the barrel was made with a hexagonal bore which was twisted. The ball was also hexagonal. For accuracy it far outstripped its contemporaries and was a favourite with sharp-shooters although it had a slightly lower rate of fire than the Enfield or Springfield. At a thousand yards its mean deviation was only fifteen inches. At five-hundred yards it was six times more accurate than the Enfield. Northern Generals Sedgwick and Lytle were supposedly shot down with Whitworths.

The Sharps Rifle. Breech loading (Falling Block) Percussion lock. One of the most famous of all early breech-loaders was the Sharps Rifle which was issued to Bredan's 1st U.S. Sharp-shooters. It could be fired six times in a minute and in their hands was accurate at seven-hundred yards. It had a ·52 inch calibre and was forty-seven inches long. Though the Federal

Government only purchased ten thousand many units were furnished with them at their State's or their own expense. There was also a thirty-nine inch carbine. One interesting version had a built-in coffee-grinder!

The Spencer Magazine Rifle. Magazine loading. Rimfire metal cartridges. Produced in musket and carbine lengths, the seven-shot Spencer was probably the most effective weapon of the war. Its rate of fire was as much as twenty rounds per minute in the hands of a trained man and its accuracy compared favourably with other weapons. Calibres varied but included the ·52 inch.

The Henry Magazine Rifle. Magazine loading. Rim fire. Benjamin Henry was the manager of Winchester's New Haven plant. In 1858 he designed the ammunition that made the Winchester possible. All the ·44 inch metal cartridges had his "H" stamped on them and for a time the weapon was known as the Henry Repeating Rifle. It had a fifteen-shot magazine beneath the barrel. A reasonably skilled man could fire an average of one shot in 2·9 seconds. With the Spencer it shared the advantage that the Confederacy was unable to manufacture the metal cartridge so that even if one of these valuable weapons was lost to the enemy it had a limited life in their hands. Though not as dependable as the Spencer, the Henry was probably the more popular because of its high rate of fire. It is doubtful if there were any of either weapon at Bull Run.

2. Artillery

The artillery used during the American Civil War was as varied as the small-arms so that this Appendix will merely serve as a guide to the general characteristics. Once again, the subject is covered in great detail, copiously illustrated, by Jack Coggins in *Arms and Equipment.*

In general all pieces conformed to the English single-trial carriage rather than the split trail of the Gribeauval System. The piece was secured to a limber by the trail. The great advantage of this system of gun and limber was that the gun carried its own supply of "ready" ammunition and could go into action and support itself until the caissons could come up. A 12 pounder limber chest held over thirty rounds for instance. It could therefore, fire for a quarter of an hour non-stop from the supply carried with it.

The type of projectile varied but may be divided into shot, shell and case. Shot was simply a solid projectile. This was normally used to destroy defences or against masses of troops. The effect of shot against troops was not only physical as the iron balls inflicted the most terrible wounds, smashing bodies and splattering blood and pulped flesh in such a manner as to weaken the morale of all in the area as it bounced like a pebble across a pond. Shells were simply hollowed projectiles of varying shape. They were filled with an explosive and fitted with a fuse which was, supposedly, ignited from the main charge. They were far from reliable but the morale effect was helpful. An improvement on the shell had been invented by Major Shrapnel RA at the time of the Napoleonic Wars. The "spherical-case" now known by his name, had the inside of the shell or case filled with musket balls and a bursting charge and could be used with devastating effect against troops.

Cannister consisted of a thin container packed with 1·5 inch iron shot or other assorted hardware — the latter more usually from the South. When used with cannister the effect of the gun was rather like that of a sawn-off shotgun. Cannister was used at close range but not over 300 yards up to which point its effect was devastating. In Napoleonic times cannister was widely used to support attacks but the great increase in small-arms range now made such a procedure extremely hazardous.

The guns which fired these projectiles were either rifled or smoothbore and, at Bull Run, muzzle-loaders. Their range was up to a mile but as they were used only for direct fire it was limited by the visibility obtaining.

The pieces themselves were classified either as "guns" — which were heavier and which had a flatter trajectory — or as "howitzers" which had a shorter barrel, greater "power-to-weight ratio" and a higher trajectory. The howitzer was not used for firing shot. Guns were also classified by weight. The standard were the 6 pounder, with a range of 1,000 yards, and the 12 pounder with a range of a mile. Probably the most generally used gun was the 12 pounder smoothbore "Napoleon", also known as the "light 12".

The guns were generally organised in six gun batteries. A 12 pounder battery would have two sections, each of two 12 pounders under a lieutenant and a howitzer section of two 24 pounder howitzers. The battery would be commanded by a captain. In action a battery front would extend to 82 yards with a similar depth from the gun line to the rear of the caissons. As with small arms at Bull Run, the types of cannon at Bull Run varied from battery to battery and we are most grateful to Mr. Coggins for supplying us with the following break-down by batteries:

Griffin's Battery D, 5th U.S. Artillery had 4 x 10 pounders and 2 x 12 pounder howitzers.

Ricketts's Battery I, 1st U.S. Artillery had 6 x 10 pounder Parrotts (rifled).

Carlisle's Battery E, 2nd U.S. Artillery had 2 x 12 pounder James Riles (sometimes listed as 13 pdrs.), 2 x 6 pounder smoothbores and 2 x 12 pounder howitzers which must have provided an ammunition supply problem.

A 2nd Rhode Island Battery had 6 x 12 pounder James Rifles (sometimes referred to as 13 pounders).

Battery E, 1st U.S. Artillery had twenty-pounder Parrotts Rifles.

Hunt's Battery was the only one which had the 12 pounder Napoleon gun-howitzer which was later to become so ubiquitous.

Ayres's Battery E, 3rd U.S. Artillery had four pieces — 10 pounder Parrotts and 6 pounder smoothbores.

Arnold's Battery D, 2nd U.S. Artillery had two James Rifles and two 6 pounders.

The total number of guns in the Union force was probably 55, the largest of which was the 30 pounder Parrott of Lt. Hains which fired the opening shot. It was abandoned during the retreat.

The Confederate pieces were all 6 pounder smoothbores — although there may have been some 12 pounder howitzers.

APPENDIX IV

Dress

WHEN the War broke out, many of the units which mobilised were social clubs of a pseudo-military type — the "chowder and marching clubs" which had sprung up to replace the standing militia. Perhaps the most outstanding were those who wore the fantastic dress of the French Zouaves with its baggy trousers, embroidered bolero and tarboosh. In this glorious costume they practised the equally ornate quick-time drill manoeuvres which they performed for public display. So admired were they that a popular song of the time stated, "My Love is a Zu-Zu-Zouave."

The dress of other units was also copied from that of other nations and we have already referred to the Scottish dress of the 79th N.Y. The N.Y. Garibaldi Guard wore a dress based on that of the Italian Bersaglieri complete with cock-plumed hat. The 2nd Ohio marched from Alexandria wearing the white cap and neck cover called the Havelock and which had been worn by British troops during the Mutiny. The Virginian cavalry had their grey jackets frogged like hussars and the Pennsylvania Lancers copied European lancer style save for the schapska. This variety was wide and it was in these outfits — more suited to a fancy-dress ball than a battlefield — that some of them went to war.

On the other hand, the official dress of both armies was much more workmanlike and practical. The dress of the Union troops was based on the fatigue dress of the Regulars. It had a short blue flannel jacket with turn down collar and five brass buttons, and the trousers were of light-blue wool. This was topped by a dark blue flannel kepi with a black peak. At this early stage this "horror of war" was unadorned save by the crossed brass sabres worn on the crown by the cavalry. The shoes were of the high type known as *brogans* which came either in pairs or in twos suitable for either foot. The shirt was supposedly grey but this seems to have been the exception rather than the rule. The wearer was paid $13.00 per month.

The Confederate foot-soldier was similarly attired but in a uniform in which grey predominated. This was supposedly based on that of the 7th New York National Guard but that is a matter for conjecture. It does, however, once again point out that, as we have seen, some Union troops wore grey and some Confederates blue. The Confederate standard dress then, consisted of grey jacket with light blue or grey trousers. The kepi had a dark blue band with the upper part the correct colour for the arm of the service; light-blue for infantry, red for artillery and yellow for the cavalry which were the same as those of the U.S. Army.

Officers of both sides wore frock-coats with the double-breasted pattern reserved for field-officers. Normally the Union wore blue and the Confederates grey, but some Confederate officers at Bull Run still retained their U.S. Army blues. Both could wear kepis but black broad-brimmed hats with cords and badges of various patterns were favoured, with or without a plume. Union officers wore rank bars on their shoulders while their Southern counterparts wore them on their collars with the addition of "chicken-gut" yellow lace Hungarian knots on their sleeves. The collar and cuffs could be the colour of Arm but were often plain.

The equipment carried varied as much between individual units as between armies but tended to conform to a pattern typical of its time and, although it was far from light we must remember that a heavy load has always been the bane of the infantryman. The essential item was a waist belt on which were carried the ammunition pouches — though sometimes a cartridge box was carried slung over the left shoulder. Having a supply of ammunition the soldier's more immediate needs were catered for by a haversack containing his rations of salt pork, etc., and by a canteen containing water if nothing stronger was available. Thus equipped he could move around the battlefield armed, fed and watered. In addition to these basics he had a knapsack or pack which contained his personal belongings, spare clothing, shoe leather, extra ammunition, shelter-tent section and similar items until it could reach a weight of twenty pounds. On top of this cumbersome load was piled a blanket or blankets, rubber sheet and greatcoat. At a later stage many men, especially the Southerners, discarded the lot and wrapped a few personal possessions in their blanket, covered it with the rubber sheet and slung it over one shoulder bandoleer-fashion.

"Reduced to a minimum, the private soldier consisted of one man, one hat, one jacket, one shirt, one pair of pants, one pair of drawers, one pair of shoes and one pair of socks. His baggage was one blanket, one rubber blanket and one haversack." But this was later.

There is a tendency for writers to comment on the wide variety of dress at Bull Run but all seem to cite the same few regiments, most of which have been mentioned at the beginning of this Appendix. It would appear, therefore, that there were probably fewer than a dozen units whose dress differed greatly from the general pattern and that most of the variations would be those of a minor, and usually decorative, nature such as the addition of coloured collars, cuffs, lacing, gaiters and so forth. It is not intended to labour the point and so at the end of this section will be found a list of some of the more unusual dress forms. Several sources have been consulted but it is quite possible that there are errors, both of omission and of commission, in these descriptions. They are, however, quite suitable for someone beginning to build a Civil War Army for wargaming.

Cavalry played no major part at Bull Run but cavalry was there and was used as is evidenced by the charge of the Virginians against the Fire Zouaves. The dress of the cavalry on both sides was, once again, basically the same. The kepi in the appropriate colours, a grey or blue jacket, usually the short shell-jacket and light-blue, tapered kerseymere trousers. Their weapons varied but would be selected from sabre, pistol or pistols and carbine. One Regiment, the 6th Pennsylvania, were armed with lances from December, 1861, to May, 1863. They were known as Rush's Lancers. The regular units of U.S. Cavalry retained the yellow braid and piping which adorned their collars and seams (Orange for the 2nd Dragoons) and similar trim was used by the Horse or Flying Artillery, in this case, of artillery red.

The gunners of ordinary field batteries wore a uniform very similar to that of the infantry but with red as the colour of Arm. The Union regulation dress specified a shell jacket with red piping round the collar and down the front edge. Brass shoulder-scales were worn. All ranks were armed with sword and pistol. The Confederate regulations stipulated a grey shell jacket with red collar, cuffs and front piping. Both sides had variations.

Mention must be made of the full dress uniform with Hardy hat and frock coat which could be piped round collar and cuff. The hat was looped up on one side and could carry a plume and badge. It is probable that some units wore this dress at Bull Run. In the authors' opinion it is a most attractive form of dress and must have looked most impressive when worn en masse by such formations as the Iron Brigade of Wisconsin when on parade with white gaiters and white gloves, headed by the live eagle mascot "Old Abe".

For the wargamer who wishes to build up a Civil War Army we would refer him to the articles by Michael Blake in *Airfix Magazine,* October 1967, November 1967, December 1967, and January 1968. These deal with all sections of the opposing forces and form a splendid basis on which to build. They give full details of converting Airfix plastic figures and are well illustrated. These Airfix figures are eminently suited to wargaming and have the great advantage of cheapness and of being available from most toy and model shops. For the Wargamer who wishes to use metal figures he will find them, for example, in the catalogues of:

Miniature Figurines. 5 Northam Road, Southampton.

This firm produces some of the cheapest metal figures in the U.K. The range includes standard infantry and cavalry as well as Zouaves, Marines and Sharpshooters.

Hinton Hunt. Rowsley, River Road, Taplow, Bucks.

This firm produces a wide range which includes guns and gunners. The General figures with maps or binoculars are particularly attractive.

Rose Miniatures. 45 Sundorne Road, Charlton, S.E.7.

This firm produces figures of both infantry and cavalry. It also makes and sells cannon in the same scale which are amongst the best available. They also produce 54mm figures of the highest quality.

Special Units

THE GARIBALDI GUARD:

Dark blue jacket and trousers. Red cuffs, collar and piping round bottom of jacket. Red piped trouser seam. Black hat. Green plumes. Black gaiters.

23rd VIRGINIA VOLUNTEERS:

Company "E", "The Brooklyn Grays". Grey frock coat. Collar edged with dark blue (black?) braid. Plain cuffs. White cross-belts and waist belt. Grey trousers with braided seam. Grey kepi with "BG" on dark blue base. Sometimes worn with oilskin cover.

ST. LOUIS NATIONAL GUARD:
Bluish-grey tunic with lace bars (black) extending about 20cm on either side of each buttonhole. Black collars. Black epaulettes with white fringes (silver for officers). Grey trousers. Grey kepi with black base. Full dress: Bearskin Grenadier cap.

12th N. Y. STATE MILITIA:
Sky-blue kepi with dark blue base. White piped seams on dark-blue jacket. Sky-blue trousers with white Hungarian knots on front thigh. Buff-yellow gaiters (high). White blanket roll on top of pack. "12 NYSM" painted on back of pack.

LOUISIANA TIGERS:
Company "B", 1st Louisiana Special Battalion. Zouave trousers of white, blue-striped, bed-ticking. Red shirt and cap. Brown jacket trimmed red. White gaiters.

1st VIRGINIA CAVALRY (Black Horse):
Grey short jackets with black collar, cuffs, piping and frogging. The frogging was of the hussar-style but spaced one row to each of the seven buttons. High black boots, Black horses.

WASHINGTON ARTILLERY (CSA):
Dark blue shell jacket with three vertical rows of buttons — nine each. Scarlet shoulder straps. Half-cuffs of scarlet with three buttons. Light blue trousers, with red stripe. Red kepi. Black belt. Gilt sword-hilt, steel scabbard.

3rd NEW JERSEY CAVALRY (1st U.S. Hussars):
Standard cavalry dress augmented by yellow collar, cuffs, piping and frogging into Hussar dress. Pill-box cap laced yellow.

LOUISIANA ZOUAVES:
Not to be confused with Tiger Rifles. Medium blue bolero festooned with coloured ornamentation. Scarlet trousers. Blue waist sash. Light blue shirt. Red fez. White gaiters.

APPENDIX V

Rules

It was orginally intended that this appendix should be a reproduction of the rules used by the authors for their re-enactment (set out in Appendix VI) but they were advised that problems of copyright would be involved and so the idea was abandoned. What is included is a description of the type of rules used and the sources of complete sets of rules in publication.

Firing
Infantry Firing was computed on a probability table in conjunction with a random number. The actual effect was varied by tactical and weapon factors. The article "Death Without Dice" which appeared in *Miniature Warfare*, Vol. 3, No. 6 explains this system. The effects of firing were deliberately kept low to reflect the low casualty rate in the actual battle.

Artillery Firing is also the subject of an article in *Miniature Warfare* by one of the authors. This was "Artillery Fire" which appeared in Vol. 1, No. 11. The system consisted of the gunners estimating the range and then casualties were computed in conjunction with a template.

Moving
Move distances were based on a scale of 1mm = 1 yard. It is not intended to reproduce the Move Tables in full as most players will almost certainly have their own. However, the march distances for infantry and cavalry are shown to give an idea of the re-enactment moves or as a basis for developing other move distances:

	Roads	Open Country	Close Country
Infantry	225 yd.	150 yd.	75 yd.
Cavalry	375 yd.	250 yd.	125 yd.

These distances refer to troops in close-order column over flat country. Appropriate additions or subtractions were made for such things as contours and varying formation.

Morale-Reaction

The reaction of troops to their circumstances was determined by obtaining a random number which in this case was done by throwing three dice. To this figure were added or subtracted points according to their circumstances. The result was obtained by comparing this number against a chart. The troops would then continue, stand, retire or run. A variation of this system is incorporated into almost all rules published.

Availability of Rules

Sets of rules for American Civil War battles are widely available and their originators usually advertise them in the two main wargaming magazines, *The Wargamer's Newsletter* and *Miniature Warfare*. Both regularly carry articles on the period. The addresses of these magazines are given below:

The Wargamer's Newsletter, 69, Hill Lane, Southampton SO1 5AD, Hampshire. The owner-editor, Don Featherstone sells rules for all periods.

Miniature Warfare, 1 Burnley Road, Stockwell, London, S.W.9.

London Wargame Section Rules, The Treasurer, L.W.S., 48 Whittell Gardens, Sydenham, LONDON S.E.26.

Bayonet, 27 Ramsgate Road, Margate, Kent.

Anwyl Agencies (Wargames), 20-24 Church Street, Oswestry, Salop.

APPENDIX VI

Re-enactment

IF one wishes to re-enact the Battle of Bull Run as a wargame then special factors must be taken into consideration when formulating or amending rules. Currently, there exist two schools of thought regarding the formulation of wargame rules. One concentrates on the "game" aspect and makes enjoyment — and often speed — the prime criterion. The other school is more concerned with attempting to draw up rules which, to quote from *Miniature Warfare,* "re-create the tactical ability and weapon capabilities of armies of a chosen period". Its criterion is realism. It is not the intention of the authors to comment on this division except to point out that the only true arbiter of a set of rules is he who plays with them. From this comfortable position, safely astride the fence, it is not proposed to put forward a set of rules, though an outline of the rules which the authors used for their re-enactment of the battle may be found at Appendix V.

Preparation

The factors which most affect any re-enactment are the size of the table on which it takes place and the terrain features represented thereon. Chapter II had already given a full description of the actual battlefield and the reader will have had chance to note the salient features in conjunction with the contour map on page 10. The next step is to decide which of these features are essential to the game before beginning to build the representative terrain. Obviously, the Run itself, the Stone Bridge, the fords, the Warrenton Pike, the Matthews Hill and the Henry Hill are almost indispensable but to what degree the contour features of the battlefield are reproduced and what area is covered is a different matter.

Based on the contour map and a study of the battlefield, a simplified map has been produced and is represented here. This map covers the whole area involved but to build it in its

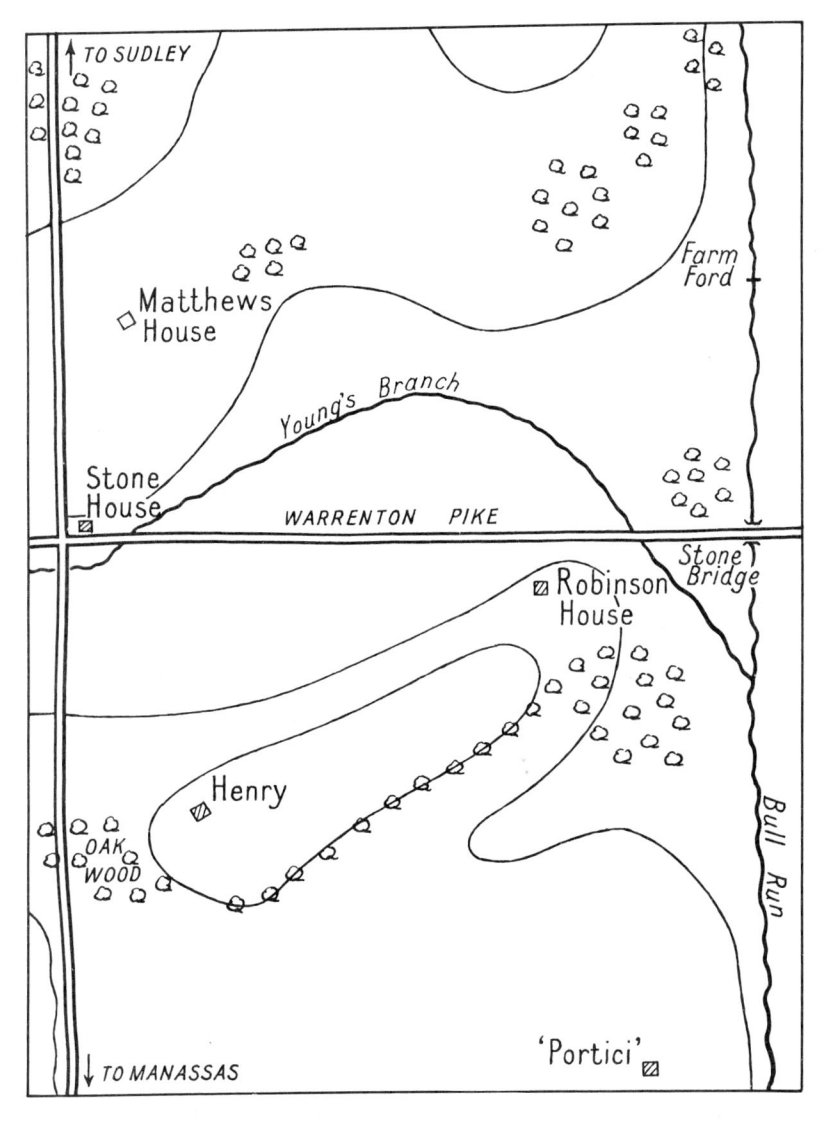

Map 13. Map of the table

entirety would require a table much larger than the authors' or that it be built on the floor. The construction, therefore, depends to such a large degree on the circumstances of the player, the room and, more especially, the time available to him, that it would be pointless to lay down definite guidance as to what part of the field should be re-constructed. However the area of the authors' table is shown on map 14 by a dotted line. It is suggested that if space is limited then the Warrenton Pike should be the

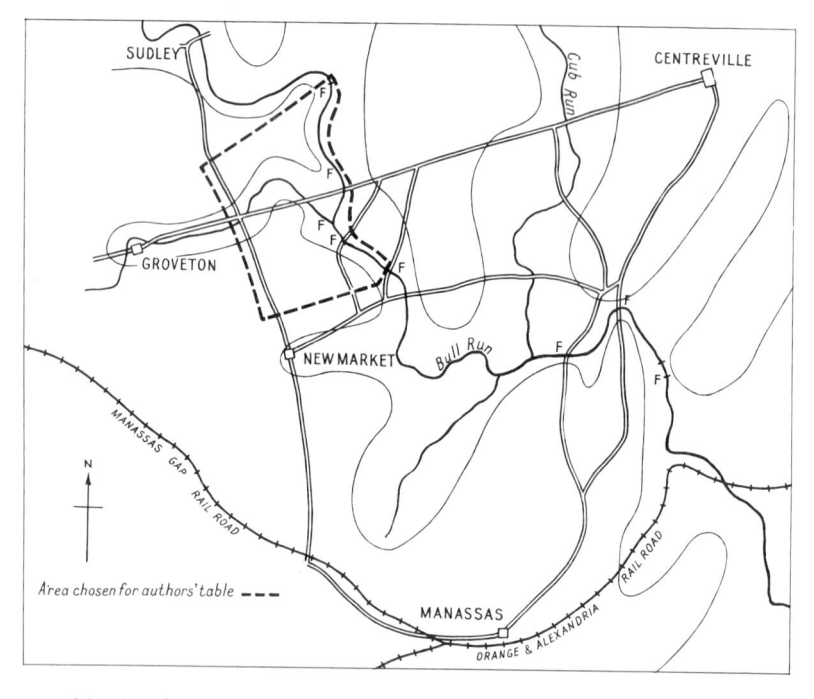

Map 14. Generalised map of essential features for setting up wargame table

lateral axis bounded on the right by the Stone Bridge and the Run. The other boundary could be to the left of the Sudley Road. The upper and lower limits would then be decided by the size of the table.

For their own re-enactment the authors used a table measuring eight feet by six feet (2.4 m x 1.8 m) which they considered a size not too difficult for the average wargamer to reproduce. Having then decided upon a ground scale of one millimetre equals one yard they proceeded to mark out their ground. The table was covered with hessian and the contours were built up with softboard. Both were painted with powder paints.

The distance between the Stone Bridge and the Stone House is approximately one mile (The Battlefield Handbook makes it longer) and so that distance taken on the table was 1750 mm or 1.75 metres. This takes up almost the whole width of the table as can be seen from Map 14 on page 82. Thus we had the table lengthwise on a north-south axis with the Warrenton Pike running east-west across the centre. The Sudley Pike, Young's Branch, the Run and the fords were then painted in. No other roads were deemed necessary. This provided a battle field almost 2,300 yards wide and extending 2,200 yards to the north, and a similar distance to the south, of its centre line. In fact one which covered the main area of the fighting.

The contours used can be seen quite plainly on Map 13 page 81. They were chosen to give a general representation of the Lewis, Matthews and Henry Features. The one specific addition was the artificial raising of the Henry Hill by another contour block. This of course was to give the Confederates the chance to establish their later "Wellingtonian" position on its reverse slope.

Though the Henry, Robinson and Stone Houses as well as Portici are marked on the map their actual importance was limited so they were reduced to "matchbox" size on the table. This meant that they could give shelter to a company but this still verges on the generous side. Close country was represented by darker stippled areas on the table surface rather than by plastic or other over-scaled trees.

Dispositions and Moves

Having constructed the table and studied the opening stage of the actual battle, the matter now turns to the commencement of the game proper and the rules which are to govern it. The choice of factors to be taken into account when formulating rules is of overriding importance at this stage.

Having decided upon a ground scale of 1 mm = 1 yd, it is reasonably easy to produce relative speeds for troops moving through different types of country. If we base our calculation on a move-time of one minute we may say that fresh infantry marching along roads travel a hundred yards in one minute and probably seventy-five or less (Jack Coggins quotes an official speed of much less) by the time they reach the battlefield. Moving across flat open ground they might cover fifty yards in the same time but in close country only twenty-five yards and all of these would be less when affected by gradients. Nevertheless we have a basic ratio of 3 : 2 : 1.

At this stage of calculation differences of opinion begin to occur but the following reasoning suits the authors. A one minute move-time would mean that a unit would take over thirty moves to get from one side of the table to the other. To allow troops to move more quickly the authors decided that a three minute move time would be suitable for their own purposes. This meant that a unit of infantry marching across open country could move approximately six inches (150 mm) in one move. A table of sample move distances may be found at Appendix V.

Firing produced a different problem and was solved by basing the number of shots fired in a move on the one minute move-time but increasing the effect so that it would be compatible with the three-minute move-time used. The system of determining fire-effect is that described in *Miniature Warfare* Vol. 3 No. 6 and is based on a random number in conjunction with an effect chart. It will not be taken as a personal insult, if, despite its excellence, the system is ignored by the reader!

When dealing with American units at any stage of the Civil War the morale factor plays a great part; even distinguished veteran regiments would sometimes refuse to attack — from circumspection rather than cowardice it should be added. At Bull Run — where two units went home before the battle started — this is even more true. Regiments would break and run easily but, paradoxically, they could often be reformed and taken back into the firing line. If anything, the Confederate troops were rather better at rallying, probably because of the experience and calibre of many of their officers. To simulate this somewhat unusual, tendency a Reaction Chart has been produced based partly on our own rules but largely on the Reaction Chart produced by Mr. Bob O'Brien and the Wargames Research Group. This forced the units involved to react according to the terrain and tactical factors obtaining when considered with a random factor.

Still considering the problem of morale, one more factor must be taken into account and this is that, when both sides have "green" troops, the morale advantage is to the defender: he is not tired, he knows where he is and can gain extra confidence by firing his rifle. His inexperienced opposite number can often see little yet is expected to advance across strange country, beset by unknown hazards and harassed by the musketry and artillery of an enemy who must surely seem braver than he. Indeed, it is not surprising that regiments broke and ran but rather, that even more of them did not move to the right about without waiting for the order.

Most of the fighting at Bull Run was done at a distance and troops only managed to get close to the enemy when they approached under cover and then, the enemy rarely stayed to keep them company. There was little, if any, serious hand-to-hand fighting and the regiments contented themselves by standing off at medium range and blasting away until one side or the other gave way.

The really zealous wargamer will most certainly study the Orders of Battle in Appendix II and make certain that the actual regiments are represented on his table so that Havelocke's 2nd Ohio appear together with the Zouaves and Highlanders of New York. This is admirable but the authors, for the sake of simplicity based their table-top units on the Brigade with the number of brigades to each division as in the actual battle. Accepting that a Brigade would have a thousand to fifteen hundred men — the actual number is debatable but the authors are not prepared to enter into debate — it could cover a front, in double line, of three hundred and fifty yards (350 mm). Using Airfix figures standing in close order it is found that one figure represents twenty-five men. Each regiment had, therefore, twenty figures. Each battery was represented by a gun on a front of seventy yards.

The plan which McDowell was forced to adopt, was very good even if rather belated and, perhaps, overambitious for inexperienced men, and there is no doubt but that it could well have succeeded — especially if the troops making the turning movement had bivouacked nearer to their start line. Beauregard's decision to concentrate to his right was also justified because it safeguarded the link from Manassas with the Shenandoah Valley and because of his intention, pre-empted though it was, of attacking McDowell's left. See map 2.

In view of this the authors decided that their game should start with the Confederate forces moving up from the Union Mills area and only one Brigade, Evans's, in the area of Stone

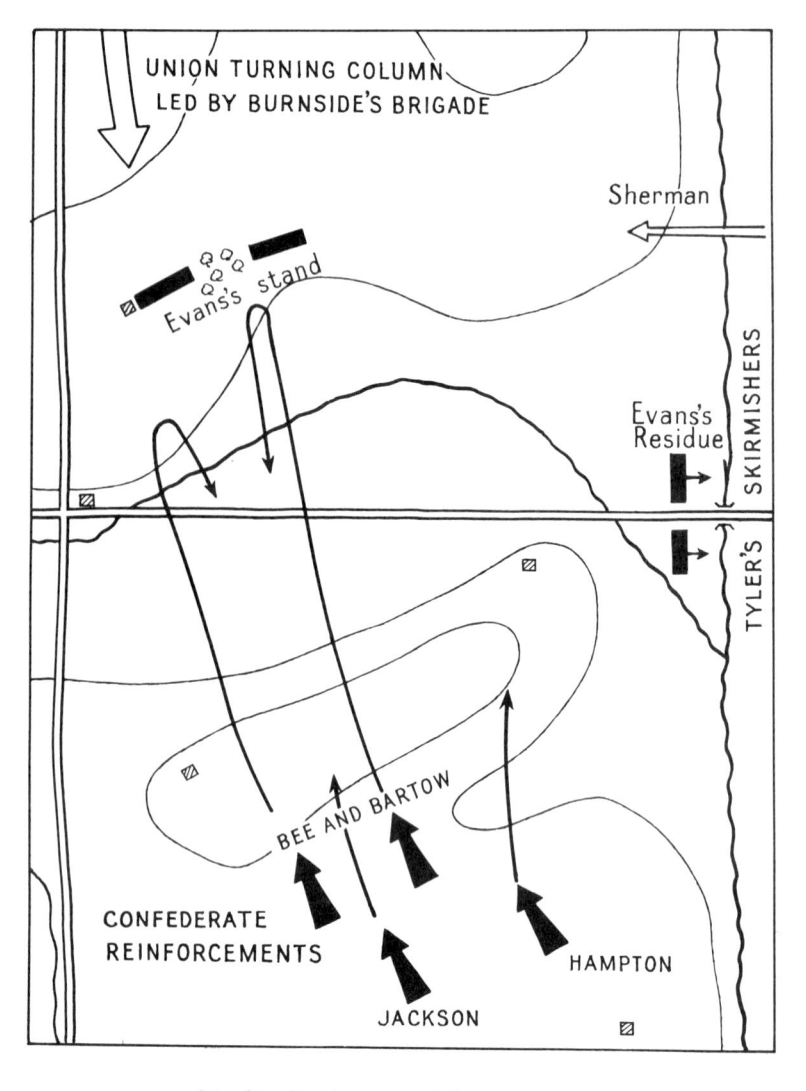

Map 15. Opening stages of the re-enactment

Bridge. Opposite Evans men at the bridge itself, Tyler's skirmishers are out but he will not move for some time. The divisions of Hunter and Heintzelman, led by Burnside's brigade, have crossed the Sudley Springs Ford and Burnside is now within rifle range of Evans's men on the high ground north of the Warrenton Pike. They exchange their initial volleys but neither gives way. The time is now 1100 hours and Bee and Bartow's forces are deployed on the Henry House hill. Behind them Jackson, yet to gain his immortal nickname, is marching hard.

Re-enactment — First Stage

When the troops are deployed on the Wargames table and the actual moving begins, any resemblance to the actual events of the battle very soon disappears unless the rules are extremely comprehensive and specially adapted, or unless the players "fudge" the results a little, or a combination of both of these occurs. We have chosen to refer to our table-top battle as a *re-enactment* as this allows us to re-shape events as needed. As each stage of the actual engagement was written up so the same stage was re-enacted on the table.

The advance of Burnside's brigade against the hastily adopted defensive position of Evans's inferior force was the opening move on the table. Because of limitations of space the Union brigade was allowed to deploy before any fire or movement took place.

The result of this initial action was strangely like that of its real-life counterpart; twice Evans's force, morale aided by the defensive bonus built into the rules, repulsed attacks and it was not until the whole of Porter's brigade was also deployed that the *Rebels* began to give ground. The possibility of Hunter's death as in the real battle, with its consequent effect on Union morale was anticipated by throwing two dice each move. If they had turned up "8" then the plastic Hunter would have turned up his plastic toes. But such was not the case.

By this time, Bee and Bartow had crossed the Young's Branch valley with their brigades and were deploying to meet Hunter's advance which was now supported by Heintzelman's two leading brigades. There ensued a steady fire-fight in which the initial casualty rate was so high that there occurred an interlude while the fire effect was considered once again. The figures we had initially used were based on those for target practice and did not allow for the slowness of loading of raw troops nor the rate of misfires one could expect. The fire-fight continued, now with a more realistic casualty rate, until Sherman's brigade could be seen appearing on the Confederate right flank. The effect of this on the reaction chart caused first one unit and then another to break off the action and retire at various speeds until the whole Southern line was in full retreat back across the stream and up the opposite slopes of the valley continually harassed by musketry and artillery fire.

To give more realism to our re-enactment, the advance of Jackson and Hampton's Legion was manipulated slightly so that they were on the Henry House ridge and the Robinson forward slopes before the disordered Confederate forces began to ascend the slopes to the east of Young's Branch followed by the Union force, now joined by Keyes's brigade of Tyler's division.

With the exception of Heintzelman's third brigade, which was accompanying Ricketts's and Griffin's batteries down the Sudley-Manassas Pike, and Sherman's force, the whole of the Union force was divided into half brigades to represent the disorder resulting from the action and the poor command. Once again this was manipulation but we feel that it was justified (see map 16).

The test would now have to be made to see whether Jackson's *Stone Wall* and the presence of the generals would add sufficient weight to tip the scales of the Reaction test so that the Southerners could stand again or whether the retreat would become a rout and the Union forces would have opened the Road to Richmond.

The scales were sufficiently weighted, this time in fact without manipulation, and so the battle could continue. As the re-enactment was specifically designed to complement the battle account of this book, manipulation once more took over and the troops were placed in suitable positions. Burnside's men moved to the rear, Ricketts and Griffin were placed on the Henry House as Imboden went back to replenish his ammunition chests. The equivalent of one whole brigade of Southerners were allowed to straggle past the Henry Hill bound for Manassas and points South. The Union forces, now in smaller groups, were massed by the crossroads and we prepared for the renewed struggle.

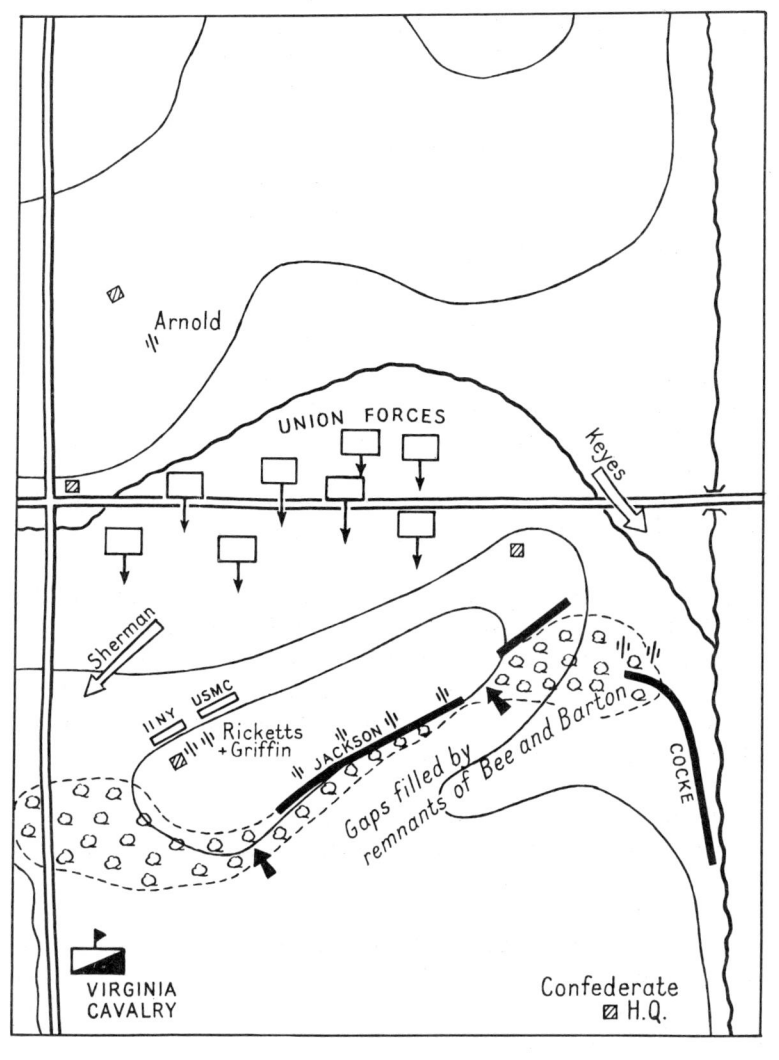

Map 16. The Union assault

Re-enactment – Second Stage

The Confederate troops were ranged along the ridge with Jackson's regiments (each regiment represented by twenty figures i.e. 500 men) forming the centre of the position and with the rallied men of Bee and Bartow supporting them. On the right the men of Wade Hampton's Legion were also in an extension of the line drawn up on the edge of the wooded area on the reverse slope of the ridge. The left flank, where the blue-coated Virginians stood, was refused slightly and to their left, behind the oak woods, stood a small force to cover the left flank and still further back, astride the Sudley-Manassas Pike, waited the 1st Virginia Cavalry of "Jeb" Stuart. In the centre front of this formidable line were placed four batteries of artillery. It was onto the mouths of these guns that the Union force was to advance.

To simulate the lack of co-ordination in the actual Union attack we had an independent spectator place the Northern regiments (in column) in random pattern with a limit of one hundred and fifty yards in front of or behind Young's Branch. Specific units were placed according to their part in the actual battle: Sherman's brigade, less one regiment, was placed on the right with orders to attack, a regiment at a time, through the oak woods against the Confederate left. Ricketts's and Griffin's batteries, covered by the New York Fire Zouaves and the USMC Bn., were placed near the Henry House. Keyes's brigade was placed on the left and ordered to move down the Young's Branch Valley against the Confederate left. In front of this brigade were the only Confederate left flank troops not on the hill – Cocke's force, less Evans, and two batteries of guns.

Though these specific forces had specific tasks assigned to them, the only orders given to the Union regimental commanders were that they were to make a general advance against the hill. Where a general officer was present he was allowed to take command of the nearest two regiments.

It might be well, at this point to look at two outstanding incidents in the actual battle and see how they turned out in the re-enactment. The first was the charge of the Black Horse against the most forward U.S. Infantry, the N.Y. Fire Zouaves. Like so many points of the re-enactment, the resemblance to the original was almost uncanny. When the charge was declared the morale of the Zouaves was tested and found to be high enough for them to stand. Their fire did not stop the Virginians who broke through but did not stop to reform and charge again.

The other incident was the devastation of Ricketts's and Griffin's batteries by the blue-jacketed 33rd Virginia. Here too the gunners failed to recognise them and the Virginians poured musketry into them at close range. The result was not as terrible as in the real incident but the guns were over-run. The only difference lay in the fact that the 33rd were supported in their advance by another regiment. The manner in which the question of recognition was decided is worth describing. At first it was intended that a dice throw should settle the matter but the innate desire of the Wargamer to improvise prevailed. Union figures were rapidly converted to Standard Bearers one with the Stars and Stripes and the other with the Confederate Battle Flag sometimes referred to as the Southern Cross. As soon as the latter was finished it was realised that at Bull Run the Confederates carried the "Stars and Bars" which was more easily confused with "Old Glory". In fact, it is suggested that Beauregard insisted on a more distinct battle ensign as a result of his experience at Bull Run. Be that as it may, the conversion stood. The two figures were placed thirty five inches (in HO scale this is approximately seventy yards — the distance to within which the Virginians approached) away from the lower mirror of a reverse periscope which is normally used for deciding matters of visibility. A team of observers then looked through the periscope and tried to distinguish which flag the figures left in front of him carried. To add to the confusion cigarette smoke was puffed across the field of vision. As it soon became obvious that absolute recognition was almost impossible, we set up the Confederate figure for the final viewing and decided to abide by that decision. The observer stated that he was certain it was a Union flag and so the batteries fell into the hands of the 33rd. Shortly after this interesting, but relatively minor affair, the first part of the major action began.

In the centre of the ridge, the advantage of Jackson's reverse slope position soon became apparent as regiment after regiment of Union infantry deployed and marched up the slope, almost unsupported by fire because of the Confederates' "hull-down" position. Finally, they crested the eminence-only to be swept with a hail of musketry from the extended grey line and from the cannister of the cannon which fronted it. The effect was always sufficient to stop them and usually enough to drive them off but for some time they slowly gained ground and eventually a vicious fire-fight developed. This failed to break the Confederates, probably because of the morale weighting given by their defensive position, and, when the Confederate commander ordered a general advance from the right flank, then the Union's precarious grip failed and they were tumbled down the hill.

On the Union left the advance had not even been as successful as this and the guns and riflemen of the Confederate force there contained Keyes's brigade so effectively that it was completely neutralised and played no further part in the action. On the Union right Sherman's attacks, restricted to one regiment at a time, were equally unsuccessful but, as each regiment fell back, the presence of Sherman and the supporting lines meant that, even despite losses, the brigade still continued to exist as a unified fighting command.

When the leading Union regiments had deployed in the dead ground below the Henry Hill they had slowed down the uncoordinated advance of those behind them, so that, while the first violent fighting was taken place, the valley floor was a scene of chaos as units sought room to deploy only to be crowded by a similar action on the part of their neighbour or disordered by the battered regiments who tried to withdraw through them. Sometimes, even, a unit would be caused to panic by the withdrawal of a disorganised regiment from the high ground. Such disorder made proper support for the forward troops impossible.

The steady advance of the Confederates began to become less steady as some units were unable to advance because losses had affected their morale. The Union forces were still not routed and many units were still in good order and ready to advance but the second attempt to take the ridge failed as disastrously as the first, which led to those regiments still left intact becoming disordered.

It was at this stage, with the Union force in great disorder and with some units actually leaving the field, that, the requisite number of moves having elapsed, Kirby Smith's force was placed on the Union right flank. All was finished.

At this stage the re-enactment was ended as it was quite obvious that the Southerners had won. It had taken almost ten hours of playing time — though much of this was occupied by the making of detailed records which were kept — and had

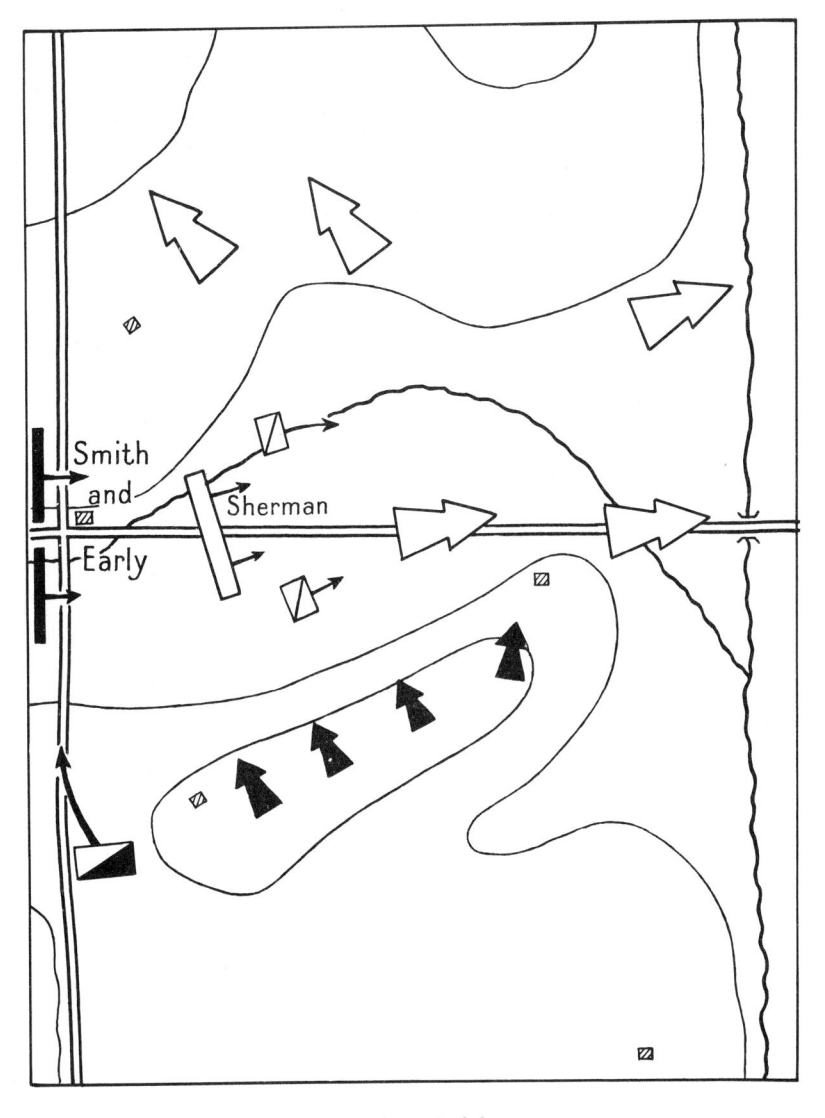

Map 17. The end of the game

ended with the Union having losses which were about a quarter higher than those of the Confederacy. The actual figures were: Union. 411 killed, 597 wounded. Confederate. 283 killed 417 wounded.

The resemblance to the actual battle was almost uncanny and it may be that a certain degree of unconscious cheating occurred — though independent observers thought not. This resemblance, it is felt, is due chiefly to the morale rules devised for the re-enactment. Had the regiments been able to fight on at the discretion of their commanders — even if only until they received 50% casualties — then the result might very well have been greatly different.

We deliberately refrained from trying any tactical movement not based on those of the battle, though such variations are discussed in Chapter VII. Despite this it seemed obvious that, had the Union attack been concerted and made with its maximum effort at one point — possibly the Confederate right — then it could well have been the Southerners who broke and ran.

APPENDIX VII

Bibliography

THE books and magazines listed in this section are those which form the basis for the material included in this book. Other works were consulted but, for reasons of space have been omitted.

BOOKS

American Civil War, Earl Miers Schenck, Golden Press Inc., N.Y., 1961.
Arms and Equipment of the Civil War, J. Coggins, Doubleday & Co. Inc., N.Y., 1962.
Book of the Gun, H. L. Peterson, Paul Hamlyn, London, 1964.
Battlefield Handbook — Manassas, F. W. Wilshin, National Park Service, Washington, 1961 (Reprint).
Battles and Leaders of the Civil War, Vol. 1, Thomas Yoseloff Inc., N.Y., 1956.
Compact History of the Civil War, R. E. and T. N. Dupuy, Collier Books, N.Y., 1962.
Compact History of the United States Marine Corps, Pierce and Hough, Hawthorn, N.Y., 1964.
Civil War Dictionary, Boatner, David McKay Co. Inc., N.Y., 1959.
Great Military Battles, edited by C. Falls, Weidenfeld and Nicholson, London, 1964.
Lincoln Finds a General, Vol. 1, K. P. Williams, Macmillan, N.Y., 1961.
Sherman, B. H. Liddell Hart, Praeger Paperbacks, N.Y., 1960.
Sherman's Memoirs, edited by E. M. Schenck. 19??.
Stonewall Jackson, G. F. R. Henderson, Longman's, London, 1961.
Weapons of the British Soldier, H. C. Rogers, Seeley Service, London, 1960.

MAGAZINES AND JOURNALS

The British Model Soldier Society *'Bulletin'*.
The Company of Military Historians'
The Company of Military Historians' *'Military Collector and Historian'*.
Tradition.
Miniature Warfare.
Wargamers' Newsletter.